Traditional Kimono Silks

Anita Yasuda

Schiffer Publishing Ltd®

4880 Lower Valley Road Atglen, Pennsylvania 19310

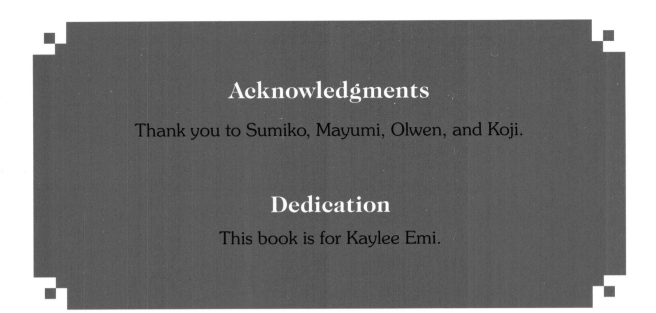

Acknowledgments

Thank you to Sumiko, Mayumi, Olwen, and Koji.

Dedication

This book is for Kaylee Emi.

Other Schiffer Books by Anita Yasuda
Japanese Children's Fabrics
Japanese Anime Linens, 1970s to Present
Hello Kitty: Forever Cute, Creative, & Collectible

Copyright © 2007 by Anita Yasuda
Library of Congress Control Number: 2007927409

Covers and book designed by: Bruce Waters
Type set in Souvenir Lt.

ISBN: 978-0-7643-2691-2
Printed in China

Published by Schiffer Publishing Ltd.
4880 Lower Valley Road
Atglen, PA 19310
Phone: (610) 593-1777; Fax: (610) 593-2002
E-mail: Info@schifferbooks.com

For the largest selection of fine reference books on this and related subjects, please visit our web site at **www.schifferbooks.com**
We are always looking for people to write books on new and related subjects. If you have an idea for a book please contact us at the above address.

This book may be purchased from the publisher.
Include $3.95 for shipping.
Please try your bookstore first.
You may write for a free catalog.

In Europe, Schiffer books are distributed by
Bushwood Books
6 Marksbury Ave.
Kew Gardens
Surrey TW9 4JF England
Phone: 44 (0) 20 8392-8585; Fax: 44 (0) 20 8392-9876
E-mail: info@bushwoodbooks.co.uk
Website: www.bushwoodbooks.co.uk
Free postage in the U.K., Europe; air mail at cost.

Contents

Preface

Fold lines, discoloration, and small pin sized holes do appear on some of the fabric swatches. These permanent marks are primarily due to improper storage and age. Some damage may have occurred when the kimono was initially disassembled, revealing a stitching line.

The word kimono itself translates as 'the thing worn'. The term kimono as used in this book's captions will encompass the different styles of kimono including *furisode, houmongi, iromotosode, yukata, tomesode, komon* and *michiyuki*.

The fabric in this book was assembled from private collections. It is primarily from the Showa period. The swatches were dated and identified with help from dealers and collectors in Japan.

Kimono swatches are available online, in small speciality stores across North America and Europe, and of course at antique markets in Japan. The prices listed beside each swatch are only meant as a guide to the reader. Neither the author nor the publisher assumes responsibility for any losses that may be incurred as a result of consulting this book.

Kimono History

Imagine a world of plum blossoms, green bamboo shoots, wisteria vines, and tiny maple leaves; a world where the flow of a mountain stream is punctuated by falling maple leaves. This is the world of the Japanese kimono, a garment inexplicably linked to images of beauty. It is perhaps one of Japan's best-known symbols.

At it's simplest, the kimono is an informal cotton robe or *yukata* used at Japanese hot baths or seen at summer festivals called *matsuri*. It's most eloquent when worn on special occasions such as weddings or coming of age ceremonies. Some of the designs are more than a thousand years old. They range from geometric lattices, diamond lozenges to peonies and chrysanthemums intermingled with figural motifs and items from daily life.

Who would have guessed that an item which meant 'clothing' to the Japanese and translates as 'the thing worn' would become an international symbol of beauty and elegance. Certainly not the people of the Jomon Period.

During the *Jomon Period* (before 300AD) clothing was a simple affair. Men and women donned loose-fitting garments fashioned out of hemp or bark. Not content with the unisex and baggy look of the *Jomon Period*, you would have to wait another couple of hundred years until the *Yayoi Period* (250BC-250AD) to see any real change.

What revolutionized clothing? A designer? An influx of good tailors? No, the weaving loom made its debut during the *Yayoi Period*. The backstrap loom may be considered primitive by today's standards but when compared to tree bark, the loom could weave fabric from vegetable fibers far superior to anything yet seen in Japan. The cloth produced was roughly the width of the human body. (Source: http://www.reconstructinghistory.com/japanese/ancient.html)

How do historians know what early people wore before 300AD? Are you thinking you can't even remember what you wore last week? Well archaeologists and historians have turned to stone cylinders called *haniwa*, for their knowledge of this ancient time (Terry, 1960). *Haniwa* are stone sculptures left on top of burial mounds. Some of the figurines are shown wearing upper and lower garments. The upper garment had short tubular sleeves (Paine & Soper, 1955, p. 6). Though it cannot be stated with 100 percent accuracy it would seem that this loose fitting upper garment was paired with an 'unsewn' lower piece, perhaps a sarong or skirt. (Source: http://www.reconstructinghistory.com/japanese/ancient.html)

With the cultivation of silk worms in Japan by Chinese settlers during the *Yamato Period* (300-550AD) we see silk being used for the first time. The colors, which dazzle us today such as rich reds or deep purples and shimmering blues, were still a long way off as the coloring process had yet to be invented. The fabric was therefore left white.

From the *Asuka Period* (552AD-645AD) to the *Nara Period* (645-794AD) sewing methods improved. Upper and lower garments were still worn but they had become longer and wider. Of great importance to the development of the kimono is what was worn underneath these garments, the *kosode*. *Kosode* means small sleeves. The 'small' refers to the sleeve opening and not the length.

The next major turning point was in the *Heian Period* (794-1192 AD) when a new technique for clothing construction was developed called the straight-line method. What did this entail? Well simply put, the fabric was cut in straight-line bocks and then sewn together. Over the next 300 years the art of layering colors developed (Dalby, *Kimono Fashioning Culture*, p. 218). Seasonal changes governed color guidelines as did affiliation to a particular political class.

The elaborate Heian kimono, with up to 12 unlined layers or *juni- hitoe*, evolved into a much simpler garment by the *Kamakura Period* (1185-1333). This was due to the decline of the aristocracy's hold on power and subsequent rise of the military class. Sumptuous layered kimonos were replaced over centuries by the simple and practical *kosode*; a garment which began as an undergarment.

The variety of color and design used on the *kosode* blossomed as the garment evolved into an outer garment. The hem line of the *kosode* which had before been tucked into the *hakama* previously, now dropped down to ankle length. By the *Momoyama Period*, *kosode* were worn by women of *every* class. Strict adherence to layered colors of kimonos to the single layered *kosode* freed designers. Elaborate designs were a way to communicate your family's status. Embroidery, tie-dye (*shibori*) and paste-resist (*yuzen*) were all used to create new and exciting textiles for the emerging merchant class. It is considered a dynamic time artistically with a resurgence of interest in the pictorial and naturalist design of the *Heian Period* combined with innovation.

Dramatic changes in dress occurred in the *Meji Period* (1868-1912) with the opening of Japan to the west and with women working outside of their homes. "The flow of western things was like a flood, and western clothes made an almost immediate impact on Japanese style of dress." (Yamanaka, *The Book of Kimono*, p.10-11). In order to distinguish Japanese dress from western dress the term kimono came into use.

The flow of trade brought goods and ideas to Japan. Cutting edge designs and fashions make their mark in the *Taisho Period* (1912-1926). With the introduction of chemical dyes and modern loom technology, an entirely new range of fabrics was created. Advances in dyeing also meant that designers were able to create larger scale compositions. Art Deco and Art Nouveau influences can be seen on kimono design from that time. These designs were not just limited to the wealthy but quickly filtered down to the masses, thanks to lower production costs. Machine-made kimonos were also relatively inexpensive to buy for the middle-class. With all these advances, the basic form of the kimono stayed the same, the only variation being sleeve length. The sleeve was somewhere between a *furisode* and the *kosode* of today.

The *Showa Period* (1926-1989) saw a major change in kimono production as silk was taxed to support the military. In terms of design, simpler layouts, which were of course less expensive to manufacture came into vogue. Even skinny sleeves were promoted as a way of supporting the war effort. After the war, kimonos were for the most part relegated to special occasion wear as people adopted western dress.

What does the future hold for kimonos? According to the All Japan Kimono Promoting Association, the industry has seen their sales drop from a high of $18.2 billion in the mid 1980s to only $5.7 billion by 2001. (USA Today 2004-09-17) What is a kimono designer to do? Some designers have turned to incorporating new images such as apples, cute puppies, and characters from animation, into their designs. These fresh ideas appeal to a new generation of kimono buyers who are looking for something inexpensive and wearable.

Kimonos may never again become daily wear, but there is still something fascinating and intrinsically beautiful in their design. A beauty that inspires artists, designers, textile enthusiasts and the average person. It is exciting to think of the fluid lines of the kimono and the rich textile history of the garment being channeled into new forms.

Japanese Historical Periods

Jomon Period, ca. 11,000 ~ 300 B.C.
Artistic high point~ sculptural deep pots and clay figurines

Yayoi Period , ca.200 B.C. ~ ca. A.D. 200
Artistic high point~ wheel turned pottery

Kofun Period, 300 ~ 552
Artistic high point~ burial mounds adorned with *haniwa*

Asuka Period, 552 ~ 645
Artistic high point~ Buddhist inspired art

Nara Period, 645-794
Artistic high point~ Buddhist and Chinese influences, period of temple building

Heian Period, 794 ~ 1185
Artistic high point~ 'golden age,' calligraphy and painting developed

Kamakura Period, 1185 ~ 1333
Artistic high point~ realistic paintings and sculptures

Muromachi Period, 1392 ~ 1573
Artistic high point~ the first ink paintings, beginning of Japanese tea ceremony

Momoyama Period, 1573 ~ 1615
Artistic high point~ extravagant textile and lacquer designs

Edo Period, 1615 ~ 1868
Artistic high point~ decorative arts flourished, woodblock prints made art available to the masses

Meiji Period, 1868 ~ 1912
Artistic high point~ opulent fabrics & dramatic motifs

Taisho Period, 1912 ~ 1926
Artistic high point~ Art Deco- and Art Nouveau-inspired textiles

Showa Period, 1926 ~ 1989
Artistic high point~ bold designs, western influences & animation age

Heisei Period, 1989 ~ present

Kimono Styles

A long-sleeved kimono may be the stereotypical image, but the truth is that this is only one style. Before the first bow or handshake, the color, design, motif, and construction of the kimono are a person's calling card. A kimono is capable of communicating your age, gender, status, and occupation, and is able to make a seasonal statement.

When is a kimono a *furisode?*

Furisode~ This bright colored silk kimono with the long flowing sleeves is a single woman's ceremonial kimono. The word means swinging sleeves. Some are richly embroidered and feature *yuzen* dyeing. The average sleeve measures 39 to 42 inches in length. A young woman would wear this style on her coming of age day or New Year's day. Other occasions include, a visit to a shrine, wedding ceremony, or reception and graduation day.

Houmongi~ This semiformal kimono is most often worn by a woman after she marries but a single woman may wear one as well. The word means visiting clothes. The *homongi* can be dyed, embroidered, a solid color or patterned. It is worn to a wedding, tea ceremony, New Year's visit to a shrine, formal party, or even a family event such as a christening.

Iromuji Kimono~ Married and unmarried women wear this semiformal style. This elegant single color kimono may have subtly woven figural patterns in the same color. They are worn to weddings, receptions, formal parties, family events, dinner etc.

Komon~ Married and unmarried women wear this semiformal style. The word means small patterns. Patterns are repeated over the entire garment. This casual kimono is worn to restaurants, visiting or shopping.

Tomesode~ Married women wear this ceremonial kimono to family functions such as weddings and receptions. The word means cut sleeves. They can be black, the type worn to a wedding or colored. Black versions are called *kurotomesode* and feature five crests; on the sleeves, chest and back. Only the bottom of the kimono skirt would have a pattern.

Tsukesage~ Married and unmarried women wear this semiformal style. The patterns on this kimono are modest with details usually only at the front and back hem lines, tops of the shoulders and on the sleeves. It is important to note that the designs always travel upwards in direction and meet at the shoulder. A special dinner or a party would be a place to wear this style of a kimono.

Tsumugi~ Married and unmarried women wear this casual style. The word means spun clothes. After individual threads are dyed, they are then woven into patterns such as checks or stripes. The pattern would not be isolated as seen on previous kimonos but cover the entire cloth. This versatile kimono has a variety of uses.

Uchikake~ Worn for a wedding. The word literally translates as hanging or covering. The bottom of the garment does drag on the ground and this hem is emphasized by a role of cotton padding at the bottom. At the actual wedding the bride would wear a white one and at the reception she would change into a brightly colored one. Lush patterns and beautiful embroidery make these pieces exceptional. Distinguishing features include long sleeves and a padding between the lining and the outer fabric.

Yukata~ Married, unmarried women, men, and children wear this casual style. The word means bathrobe. They are always unlined, made of cotton, cotton/poly blends, linen or hemp. Navy and white are the traditional colors but now they are available in a wide range of colors. This style would most often be worn to a summer festival (*matsuri*), at a hot spring resort (*onsen*) or even after a bath.

Men

Kimonos for men are usually more subdued than women's kimonos with little or no patterning (see *Yamanaka, The Book of Kimono*, p. 102). Kimonos made from wool or spun silk in shades of brown and grey are common choices for informal kimonos. In the summer months, *yukatas* are the popular choice. For a formal occasion a crested kimono, or *kuro-montsuki,* is worn.

Kuro-montsuki~ This ceremonial kimono is black with a family crest, or *mon*. The crest is placed on the kimono in five places, back of both sleeves, right and left breast, and on the back mid-seam.

*For even more information on kimono trends and industry forecasts there is a national organization in Japan called the All Japan Kimono Promoting Association. The website, in Japanese, is: http://www.kimono-net.or.jp/

Chapter One
Cherry Blossoms

Detail of palace doll with fishing rod and carp. It is common to find palace dolls shown with objects associated with famous characters from Japanese history, fables or even the theater. Here the doll represents *Ebisu* the daily god of provision. *Ebisu* was symbolized by a fishing pole and a carp. (Source: Alan Pate http://www.akanezumiya. com/gal_artinfocus.html)

Girl's undergarment (*juban*). Silk dyed print. Showa Period, 13 x 7 in. A playfudesign featuring imperial palace dolls (*gosho ningyo).* The doll's small size (1") compliments the delicatepink ground color. $5~10. *Palace dolls are sometimes referred to as *karako* or 'Chinese children'. The next five pictures are from this undergarment.

Detail of palace doll as referee (*gyoji*) at a sumo match. The doll holds a solid wooden fan (*gunbai*) in his right hand. The *gunbai* is used in pre bout ritual and to point to the winner's side at the end of the match.

Detail of palace doll.

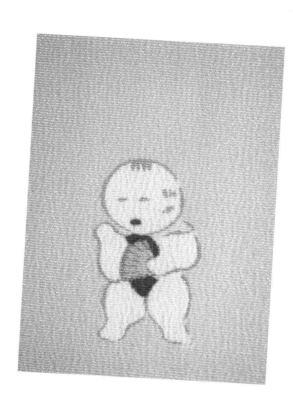

Detail of palace doll with a fan.

Detail of palace doll.

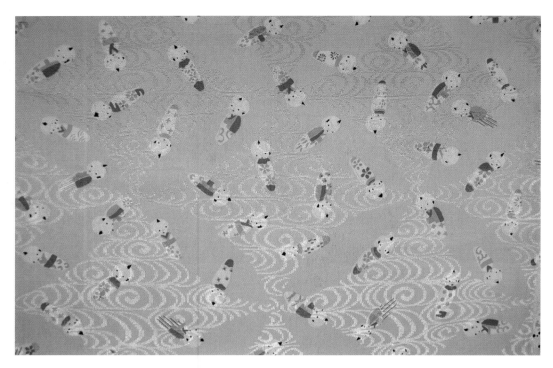

Girl's undergarment (*juban*). Silk dyed print. Showa Period, 13 x 9. An elegant pattern of *Kokeshi* dolls and interconnecting diamond motifs. The pattern repeats every inch. The diamond motif itself is made up of elaborate arabesques. There are twelve different varieties of dolls on this small piece. Each doll measures 1" in height. Some of the motifs used on the body of the doll include the coma (*tomoe*) plum blossoms (*ume*) and semicircular waves (*seigaiha*). The *kokeshi* doll is a hand-painted wooden doll with a 150-year history. The doll originated in the Togatta/Miyagi region of Japan. It is thought that they started to be produced in the late *Edo* period.

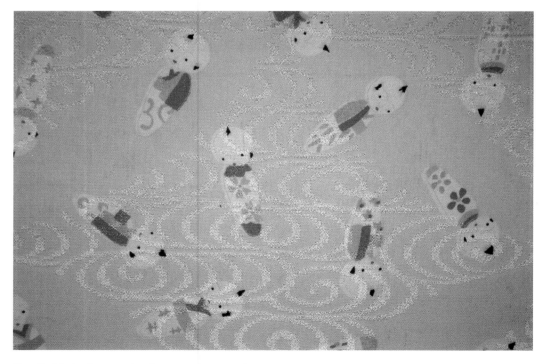

Detail of *kokeshi* grouping from previous textile.

Girl's undergarment (*juban*). Silk dyed print. Showa Period, 13 x 9. A playful design of tops (*koma*). The small tops are 1" in diameter and the larger top measures 2.5". Stripes, arabesques and flowers are all used to decorate the tops.

More tops each with an intricate design from previous textile.

The movement of the tops is wonderfully communicated through the design of the winding red ribbon.

Detail of red chrysanthemum embellished top from previous textile.

Girl's kimono remnant. Silk dyed print. Showa Period, 13 x 8.5. Overlapping fan motifs, each with auspicious motifs, create an elaborate design. In the top right corner is a fan with a soaring crane design. On the left is one adorned with two peony blossoms. Adding even more depth to this piece is the addition of the *kanoko* dot pattern in blue in the lower right corner. The light blue *kanoko* dot design serves to draw the eye to the coordinating blue silk threads in the fan motifs, therefore creating an element of movement.

tsuzumi) motif adorns the fan in the forefront of the gain the amount of detail on this piece with the ad- *kanonko* dot designs in red on the drum's surface. right of the central image reveals an *asanoha* pat- from previous textile.

A royal carriage or ox cart and semicircular wave detai form an elegant composition. Motifs from daily life suc were considered not dignified enough to be used as a (motif until the Edo period. (Mizoguchi, 1973, 119)

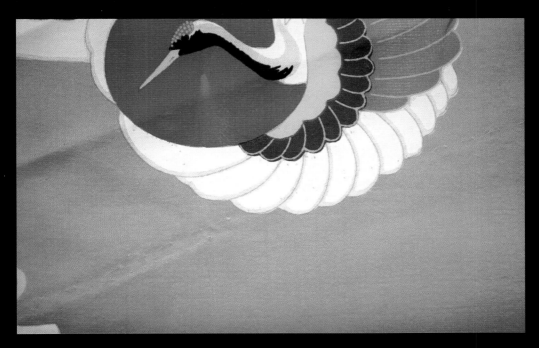

Girl's kimono fragment. Synthetic silk blend with a dyed print. Showa Period, 13 x 7. A circle crane (*tsurumaru*)motif on silk. Cranes along with turtles are symbols of longevity and as such are popular motifs on children's kimonos.

Close-up of the neck and wings of the crane. The truncated image measures 2.5".

Girl's kimono fragment. Synthetic silk blend with a dyed print. Showa Period, 7 x 6. Vibrant butterfly motif finely outlined in silver metallic thread. Circles, half moons and tear drops add drama to this stylized form.

Crest with *double petal* plum blossom. Each petal of the plum has a small *kanoko* dot detail.

In this new version of a family crest, the classic image of bamboo (*take*) takes on a decidedly modern look with the choice of a heavy white border. The result is an awkward composition. The crest measures 2.5".

Young girl's kimono remnant. Cotton blend with a dyed print. Showa Period, 4 x 4. A large floral *tsuzu* with elaborate gold hanger and paper crane *(oritsuru)* creates an elaborate design. The wings of the crane contain many smaller geometric motifs such as *asanoha*.

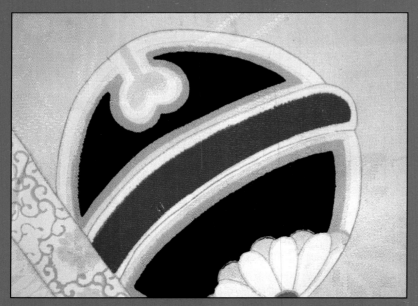

Girl's kimono fragment. Silk dyed print with damask effect. Showa Period, 10 x 6.5. The choice of black for the *tsuzu* against the soft pink ground color makes for a sharp contrast. The following two pictures are from this kimono.

Detail of the chrysanthemum motif on the pink ground color.

Double petal chrysanthemum, green and red bells *(tsuzu)*. Note: Here is a quick way to tell the difference between a *temari* and a *tsuzu* motif. If you look closely at a bell motif there will always be a small section cut out at the bottom, like a keyhole. Sometimes this part is dyed yellow.

Red bell with gold holder in chrysanthemum design. The design of the holder is echoed in the subtle chrysanthemum pattern on pink ground color. Remnant from previous textile.

Girl's kimono fragment. Silk dyed print with damask effect. Showa Period, 14 x 6.5. White bell (4.5") with a red band and gold hanger. Just before midnight on New Year's Eve in Japan, temple bells are rung continuously into the early hours of New Years Day for a total of 108 times. This special ringing of the bell is called *Joya no kane* in Japanese and children try and stay up just to hear the sound.

Girl's kimono fragment. Silk dyed print with damask effect. Showa Period, 14.5 x 6.5. An elegant *temari* (6.5") with interwoven multicolored ribbons. The flow of the ribbons creates a design full of movement and energy. *Crease line due to age.

Girl's kimono remnant. Silk crepe (*kinsha*) with a dyed print. Showa Period, 13 x 7. Dynamic chrysanthemum petals. Some petals contain smaller images of blossoms. Adding depth to the design is the black and gold center of the chrysanthemum that is raised.

Girl's kimono remnant. Silk dyed print with damask effect and metallic thread detailing. Showa Period, 13.5 x 7. A band of pink and green, perhaps belonging to a larger ribbon motif creates a powerful effect. Adding another dimension to this design is the beautiful snow pattern (*yukiwa*) on the pink ground color. *Crease line due to age.*

Girl's kimono remnant. Silk dyed print with damask effect and metallic thread detailing. Showa Period, 13.5 x 7. Gold metallic thread outlines petals of an elaborate plum blossom.

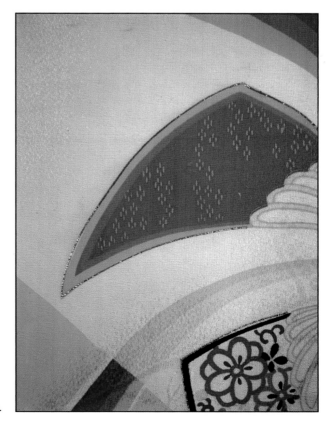

Detail of *kanoko* dot design on ribbon from previous textile.

Girl's kimono remnant. Silk dyed print with damask effect and metallic thread detailing. Showa Period, 13 x 7. A bold chrysanthemum motif and sweeping ribbons. Tortoise shell hexagons (*kikko*) on the top ribbon are as vividly colored as the ribbons. Small paulownia flowers placed beside the hexagons make an interesting contrast between geometric and naturalistic form.

Girl's kimono remnant. Silk dyed print with damask effect. Showa Period, 14 x 7. Twisted plum blossoms *(nejiume)* create an exuberant design. In the petals are smaller blossoms and wave *(seigaiha)* motifs. In the upper left corner are *kanoko* dot and *sayagata* patterns. It is possible to see the evolution of this design from a single blossom decorative motif in the Kamakura Period to double blossom and even twisted variations on family crests during the Edo and Meji periods. (Mizoguchi, 1973, 135)

Girl's kimono remnant. Silk dyed print. Showa Period, 7 x 6.5. A beautiful layered design of chrysanthemums against a carpet of diamond shaped flowers. The flowers are enclosed within a hexagonal tortoise shell (*kikko*) motif. This pattern is called *kikko-hanabishi*. "This pattern achieved its greatest popularity during the *Heian* period." (Mizoguchi, 1973, 54)

Stylized medallions, an ornate *temari* and colorful blossoms including a plum make a gorgeous design. 7 x 6.5. Remnant from same kimono as previous.

Young woman's kimono remnant. Silk dyed print with damask effect. Showa Period, 14 x 7. A vivid design with chrysanthemums, small blossoms and ribbons. Again we see the contrast between the sharp geometric lines in the bands of color behind the flowers and the curved form of the petals.

Detail of shading on chrysanthemum petals from previous textile.

Woman's kimono fragment. Silk crepe (*kinsha*) dyed print. Showa Period, 4.5. x 3.5. A twisted plum (*neji-ume*) motif with citrine green outline and contrasting yellow details.

Young woman's kimono. Silk dyed print with damask effect and metallic thread details. Showa Period, 13 x 6.5. Foliage and small colorful chrysanthemums. The semicircular wave design in relief echoes the larger curves of the foliage.

Young woman's kimono remnant. Silk dyed print. Showa Period, 13 x 6.5. Chrysanthemums with arabesque design and bands of brilliant green and yellow. The intertwined cords create energy and movement on the piece.

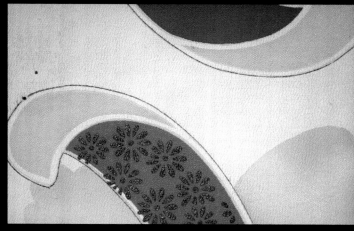

Young woman's kimono remnant. Silk dyed print with damask effect. Showa Period, 13 x 6.5. Ribbons on stylized cloud background. *Crease line and mark due to age.*

Woman's kimono fragment. Silk dyed print with metallic thread details. Showa Period, 6 x 5.5. The curve of a stylized chrysanthemum petal is accentuated with small blossoms in gold.

Striking chrysanthemum motif (3.5"). The triple layers of petals in black with gold geometric details add dimension to the blossom. 7 x 6.5. Remnant from previous textile.

Young woman's kimono remnant. Silk dyed print with damask effect and metallic thread details. Showa Period, 7 x 6.5. Layers of petals, some with geometric designs serve to highlight the beauty of the red chrysanthemum center.

Young woman's kimono fragment. Silk dyed print with damask effect. Showa Period, 7 x 6.5. Bell and chrysanthemum with dramatic petals in shades of green, red, white and black.

Woman's kimono fragment. Silk crepe print with metallic thread details. Showa Period, 7 x 6.5. Chrysanthemums and silhouette.

Young woman's kimono fragment. Silk dyed print with damask effect. Showa Period, 13 x 6.5. Chrysanthemum (4") with ribbons and smaller floral motifs.

Young woman's kimono remnant. Silk dyed print with damask effect. Showa Period, 7 x 6.5. Double petal chrysanthemum (3").

Girl's kimono remnant. Silk dyed print with damask effect. Showa Period, 15 x 6.5. Chrysanthemum with stylized petals surrounded by colorful ribbons. Subtle leaf motifs bring dimension to the pink ground color.

Woman's kimono remnant. Silk dyed print. Showa Period, 6 x 6. A red bridge motif peaks out from the cluster of blossoms and pine tree motifs.

Maple leaf and bamboo motifs shown here against stylized grey mountains. 6 x 6. Remnant from previous textile.

Paulownia, peonies and assorted blossoms. 6 x 4.5.

Woman's kimono remnant. Silk crepe dyed print with metallic thread details. Showa Period, 6 x 4. Flower grouping. The following three pictures are from this kimono.

Maple leaf and ribbon motifs. 6 x 4.

Ribbons, blossom and cloud detail in the lower right-hand corner. 6 x 4.

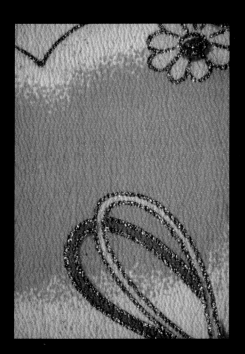

Blossom and ribbon detail. 6 x 4.

Young woman's kimono lining (*juban*) remnant. Cotton dyed print. Showa Period, 13 x 7. Stylized plum blossom with *a kanoko* dot lattice pattern on the petals. *Discoloring due to age*

Young woman's kimono fragment. Silk dyed print with damask effect. Showa Period, 12.5 x 6.5. Exquisite peony bloom in rich yellow against a solid pink ground color.

Young girl's kimono remnant. Silk dyed print. Showa Period, 13.5 x 7. A large circular motif with plum blossom, *kanoko* dots and bamboo motifs. The circle is part of a larger hand drum motif.

Blossoms in rich shades of crimson, pink, blue and yellow on a circular motif. Remnant from previous kimono.

Young woman's kimono remnant. Silk dyed print with damask effect and gold metallic details. Showa Period, 5 x 3.5. Wheel and chrysanthemum design.

A tortoise shell lattice pattern with a stylized flower (*kikko-hanabishi*). The cloud motifs around the lattice are highlighted with gold metallic thread. 5 x 3.5. Remnant from previous textile.

Detail of clouds. Remnant from same kimono as previous. 5 x 3.5. *Crease due to age.*

Young woman's kimono remnant. Silk dyed print with damask effect. Showa Period, 6.5 x 5. Peony and assorted blossoms make for a cheerful piece.

Remnant from previous kimono. Three hexagons with stylized plum motifs. A family crest design here revitalized with fresh colors giving the crest an almost cartoon like quality.

Young woman's kimono remnant. Silk dyed print with damask effect. Showa Period, 6 x 4.5. Partial hexagon and blossom.

A cluster of colorful triple diamond motifs. Remnant from previous textile.

Young woman's kimono remnant. Silk dyed print with damask effect. Showa Period, 6.5 x 5. Elaborate fan with plum blossom, maple leaf and bamboo motifs.

Woman's kimono remnant. Silk dyed print. Showa Period, 7 x 6. An elegant winter theme with pine, bamboo and plum (*sho-chiku bai*) motifs on a deep pink ground color. The following two pictures are from this kimono.

Detail of maple leaves and pine trees. 5 x 6.

Detail of royal carriage or ox cart decorated with white cranes. 5 x 6.

Woman's kimono remnant. Cotton woven design. Showa Period, 7 x 6. Elegant blooms. The following three pictures are from this kimono.

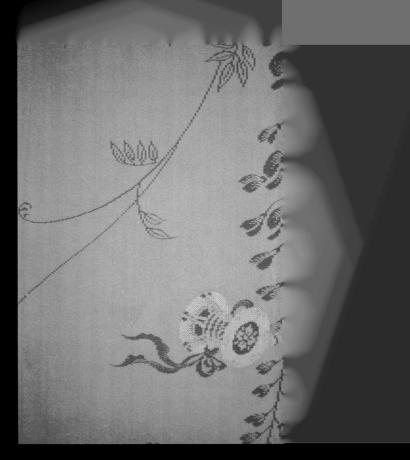

Hand drum (*tsuzumi*) motif. (2.5") 7 x 6.

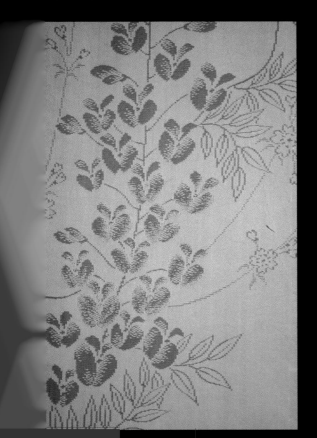

...aves. 7 x 6.

Young woman's kimono remnant. Silk dyed print. Showa Period, 5 x 4. Chrysanthemums, plum blossoms and maple leaves are gently scattered over the pink and cream ground color.

Young woman's kimono remnant. Silk dyed print with damask effect. Showa Period, 14 x 6.5. Chrysanthemums, maple leaves and clouds frame the image of a bridge.

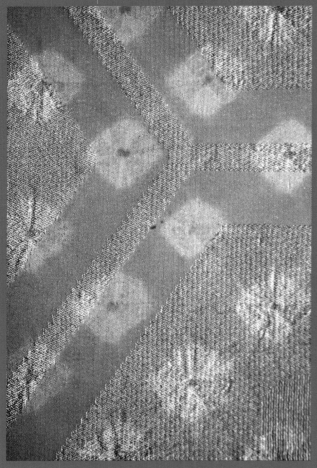

Girl's undergarment (*juban*) remnant. Silk *shibori*-like print with a damask *effect*. Showa Period, 4.5 x 4.

Young girl's kimono lining (*juban*) remnant. Cotton dyed print. Showa Period, 5 x 2. Plum blossom and small blue camellia motif. *Crease is due to age.*

Plum blossoms. 5 x 2. Remnant from previous textile.

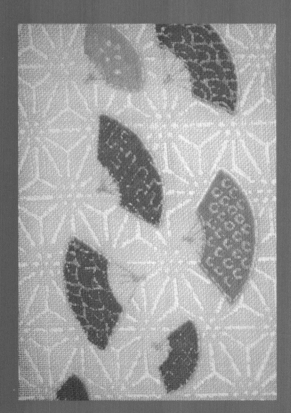

Woman's kimono lining (*juban*) remnant. Cotton dyed print. Showa Period, 7.5 x 3. Tiny fans (5") are scattered over the *asanoha* patterned background.

Patterns on fans include sayagata, *kanoko* dot, and plum blossom. 7.5 x 3. Remnant from previous textile. *Discoloring due to age.*

39

Young woman's kimono lining (*juban*) remnant. Silk dyed print. Showa Period, 7.5 x 3. White blossoms with a bold red center on soft pink ground color. *Crease due to age.*

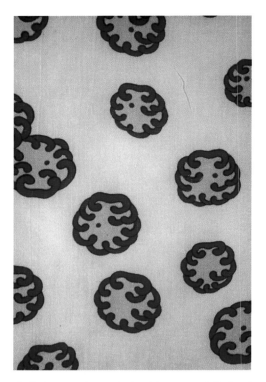

Girl's kimono lining (*juban*) remnant. Silk dyed print. Showa Period, 7.5 x 3. A stylized motif.

Woman's kimono remnant. Silk dyed print. Showa Period, 7.5 x 3. Blue and purple chrysanthemums.

Woman's kimono remnant. Silk dyed print with damask effect. Showa Period, 7.5 x 3. Bold flower with a red outline.

Woman's kimono remnant. Silk synthetic blend dyed print with metallic detailing. Showa Period, 6.5 x 4. Blossoms and foliage.

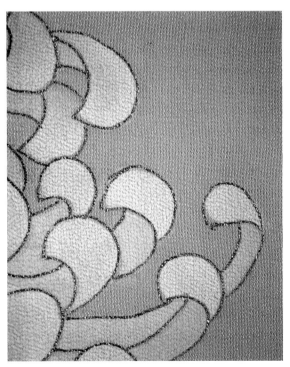

Woman's kimono remnant. Silk synthetic blend. Crepe dyed print. Showa Period, 7 x 6. Stylized chrysanthemum petals.

Detail of a petal from previous textile. 7 x 6.

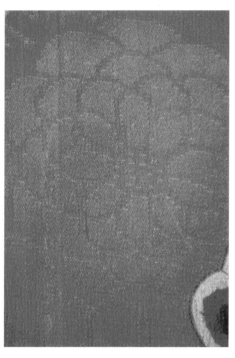

Woman's kimono remnant. Synthetic dyed print. Showa Period, 7 x 6. White blossom and leaves.

Woman's kimono remnant. Silk dyed print with damask effect. Showa Period, 6 x 3. Large blossom in relief. *Crease due to age.*

Woman's kimono lining (*juban*) remnant. Silk dyed print. Showa Period, 7 x 6.5.*Crease due to age.*

Young girl's kimono lining (*juban*) remnant. Silk blend dyed print. Showa Period, 13.5 x 7. A *kanoko dot* pattern in pale pink and white.

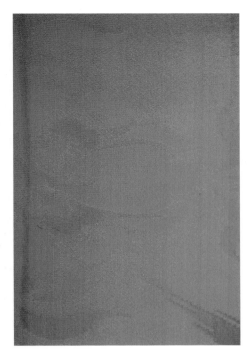

Woman's *iromuji* kimono remnant. Silk dyed print with damask *effect*. Showa Period, 10 x 7.

Woman's *iromuji* kimono remnant. Silk dyed print. Showa Period, 13.5 x 7. *Sayagata* pattern with blossoms. The *sayagata* pattern combined with blossoms such as chrysanthemums or plums can be traced back to the *Edo* period. *Crease due to age*

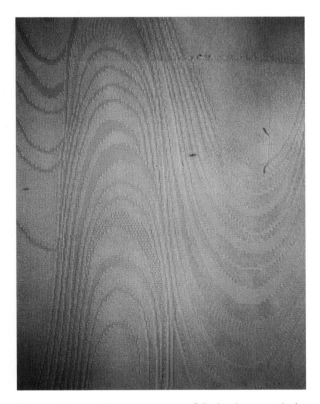

Woman's *iromuji* kimono remnant. Silk dyed print with damask effect. Showa Period, 13.5 x 7. Elegant wave design.

Woman's *iromuji* kimono remnant. Silk blend dyed print with damask *effect*. Showa Period, 4 x 4. A maple leaf motif.

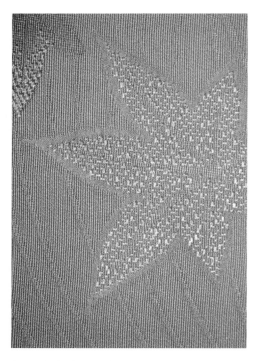

A maple leaf motif from previous textile.

Woman's *iromuji* kimono remnant. Silk crepe dyed print. Showa Period, 13.5 x 7. This raised design is composed of pine trees and streams.

Ladies kimono remnant. Silk dyed print. Showa Period, 13.5 x 7. A sophisticated *sayagata* pattern in subtle shades of pink and cream.

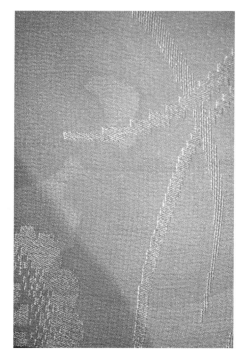

Woman's kimono lining (*juban*). Silk dyed print. Showa Period, 13.5 x 7. *Mark due to water damage.*

Chapter Two
Peonies

Girl's kimono remnant. Silk dyed print. Showa Period, 7 x 6. Blossoms and leaves against a pink cloud motif.

Flowers including peonies from previous textile.

Girl's kimono remnant. Silk dyed print. Showa Period, 14.5 x 6. Flower cart *(hana guruma)* in an upper medallion with vivid peony blossom. A tasseled rope motif from the cart connects the two medallions.

Girl's kimono remnant. Silk dyed print. Showa Period, 14 x 6.4. Chrysanthemums, assorted blossoms, and a *kanako* dot pattern. **Fold line and discoloring due to age.*

Girl's kimono remnant. Cotton dyed print. Showa Period, 7 x 6. Camellia, peony and assorted blossoms. The truncated image in the left corner features plum blossoms, *kanoko* dot pattern and a tortoise shell (*kikko*) designs all in a space less than two inches long.

Woman's kimono fragment. Silk dyed print. Showa Period, 11 x 6. Bamboo and blossoms on a fan motif. *Discoloring is due to age.*

Young woman's kimono remnant. Silk dyed print. Showa Period, 5 x 6.5. Circle of flowers with *kanoko* dot design beneath.

Young woman's kimono remnant. Silk crepe dyed print. Showa Period, 7 x 6.5. A cluster of flowers. By varying the petal design from *a kanoko* dot to solid to neutral white, the overall effect is quite light.

Peonies, bamboo and plum motifs are almost overwhelmed by the choice of turquoise blue for accenting the foliage. Remnant from previous textile.

Woman's kimono fragment. Silk dyed print with damask effect. Showa Period, 5 x 3.5. Large red and white chrysanthemum on solid red ground color.

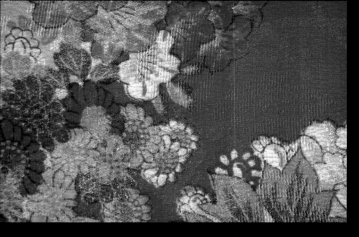

Woman's kimono fragment. Silk dyed print with damask effect. Showa Period, 6.5 x 4. Blossoms.

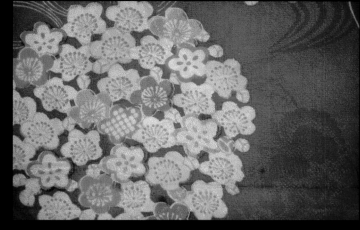

Woman's kimono fragment. Silk dyed print with damask effect. Showa Period, 6.5 x 4.5. An elegant plum blossom circular motif.

Girl's kimono remnant. Silk dyed print with damask effect. Showa Period, 6.5 x 4. A white peony blossom. It is interesting to note that the peony was once considered exotic and foreign around Heian Period before cultivation of this flower in Japan. (Mizoguchi, 1973, 49)

Winding ribbons and blossoms. A ribbon motif and subtle *ta-suki* pattern feature on the red ground color. 6.5 x 4. Remnant from previous textile.

A white peony and blue fan motif. 6.5 x 4. Remnant from previous textile.

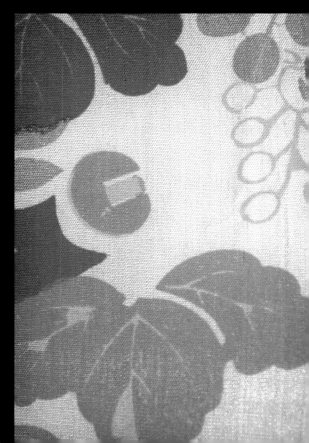

Young woman's kimono fragment. Silk print design. Showa Period, 13.5 x 7. A spring theme kimono with wisteria and paulownia blossoms.

Detail of petals on paulownia from previous textile.

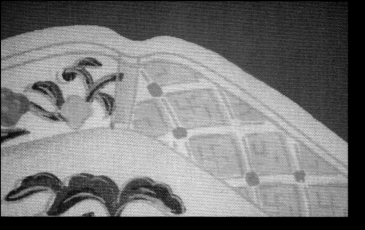

Woman's kimono fragment. Silk dyed print. Showa Period. 5 x 6.5. Only the border of a medallion remains with a lattice pattern.

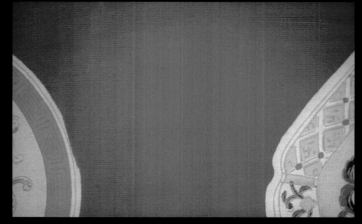

In this separate fragment it is possible to make out another medallion with a solid orange border. 7 x 6.5. Remnant from same kimono as previous.

Woman's kimono fragment. Silk dyed print. Showa Period. 7 x 6.5. An overall pattern of maple leaf motifs.

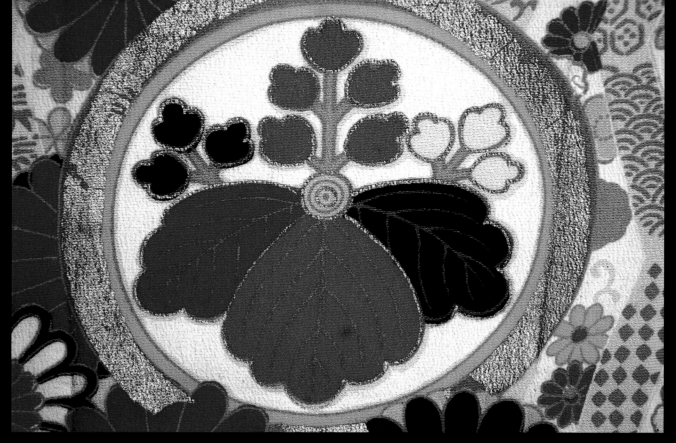

Woman's kimono fragment. Silk dyed print. Showa Period. 7.5 x 6. Large crest design with a paulownia motif. Gold waves, hexagons and diamonds are a few of the designs to the left of the central motif.

Chrysanthemum with metallic details and *tome* design on a partial crest. 4 x 6. Remnant from previous textile.

Bold chrysanthemums, stylized *tome* and gold bamboo motifs. Remnant from kimono same as previous. 7.5 x 6.

Young girl's kimono fragment. Silk dyed print. Showa Period, 13 x 6.5. Layered petals of a chrysanthemum with metallic details.

Young Woman's kimono fragment. Silk dyed print with metallic details. Showa Period, 5 x 6.5. Bands of white and red create a strong visual effect. Multicolored chrysanthemums, leaves and metallic clouds also feature.

Detail of leaf design from previous textile. 5 x 6.5.

Flowers, a leaf and a small *kanoko* dot design. 4 x 6.5. Remnant from previous textile.

Woman's kimono remnant. Silk dyed print. Showa Period, 7 x 6.5. Chrysanthemums and gold arabesque patterns.

Woman's kimono fragment. Silk crepe print with gold metallic detailing. Showa Period, 17 x 7. A dramatic wheel motif. The use of color to highlight the individual spokes creates a three-dimensional image. *Crease due to age.*

A curtain (*maku*) motif with flowers, lattice and even an hourglass (*tatewaku*) design in the lower central panel. Remnant from previous textile.

Woman's kimono fragment. Silk dyed print with damask effect. Showa Period, 7 x 6. An elaborate fan, ribbon and blue *kanoko dot* pattern. *Crease and discoloring due to age.*

Woman's kimono fragment. Synthetic dyed print.
Showa Period, 13 x 7. Interesting juxtaposition of linear
and floral motifs.

Young Woman's kimono lining (*juban*) fragment. Silk
dyed print. Showa Period, 14 x 7. A red *kanoko* dot
pattern with large pink rose.

Woman's kimono remnant. Silk crepe (*kinsha*) dyed print. Showa Period, 7 x 6.5. A striking red lattice provides a dramatic backdrop to red, black, green and grey pines.

Detail of flowers from previous textile. 7 x 6.5.

Woman's kimono lining (*juban*) remnant. Silk dyed print. Showa Period, 7 x 6. A bold *kanoko* dot pattern.

Woman's kimono lining (*juban*) remnant. Silk dyed print. Showa Period, 7 x 6.5. *Kanoko* dot.

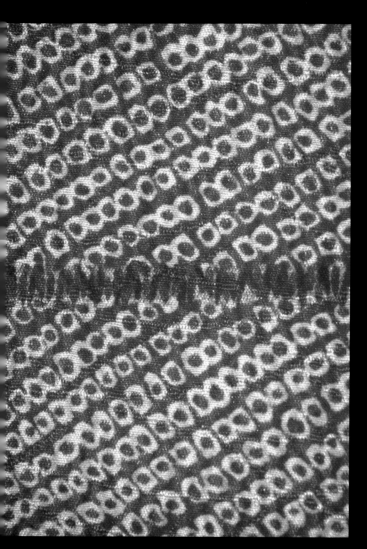

Woman's kimono lining (*juban*) remnant. A silk *kanoko shibori* pattern. Showa Period, 7 x 6.5.

Remnant previous kimono. 7 x 6.5.

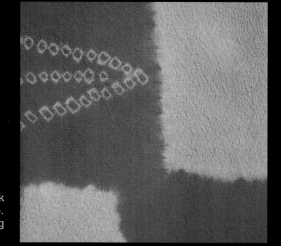

Woman's kimono fragment. Silk
shibori print. Showa Period, 6 x 5.5.
A *kanoko* dot pattern and alternating
squares of red and cream.

Girl's kimono remnant. Silk dyed print.
Showa Period. 7 x 7. *A kanoko* dot pattern. blossoms and ribbon.

Blossoms, persimmon with *kanoko* dot design. 7 x 7. Remnant from previous kimono.

Girl's kimono remnant. Silk dyed print. Showa Period, 13 x 6.5. A *kanoko* dot pattern with cords. *Crease due to age.*

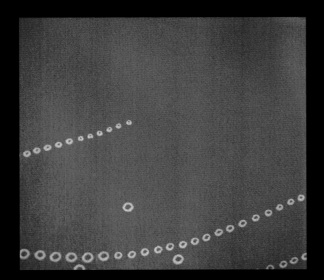

Girl's kimono lining (*juban*) remnant. Silk dyed print.
Showa Period, 6 x 5.5. Small *kanoko* dot design.

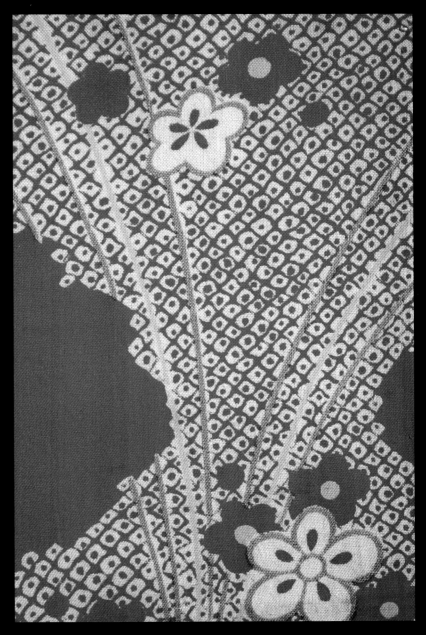

Girl's kimono remnant. Silk dyed print. Showa Period, 6 x
5.5. Overall *kanoko* dot design, plum blossoms and ribbons.

Ladies kimono fragment. Silk dyed print. Showa Period, 7 x 6.5.
A *kanoko* dot pattern. Partial medallion with floral component.

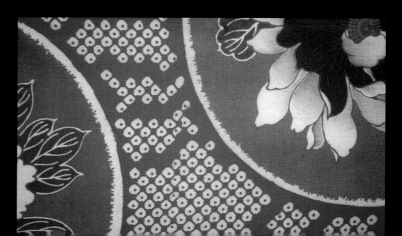

Two partial medallions. 7 x 6.5.
Remnant from previous kimono.

Ladies kimono remnant. Silk dyed print with damask effect. Showa Period, 7 x 6.5. Fan with *kanoko* dot pattern and large chrysanthemum motif. A beautiful crane and lattice design add richness to the pink ground color.

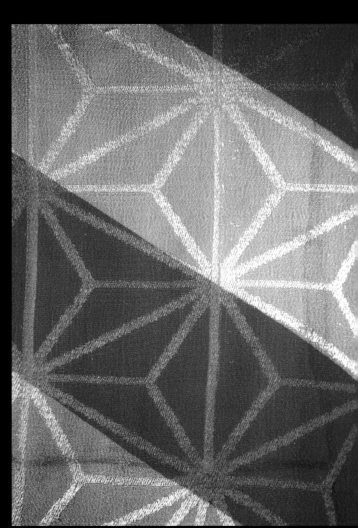

Detail of *asanoha* pattern.

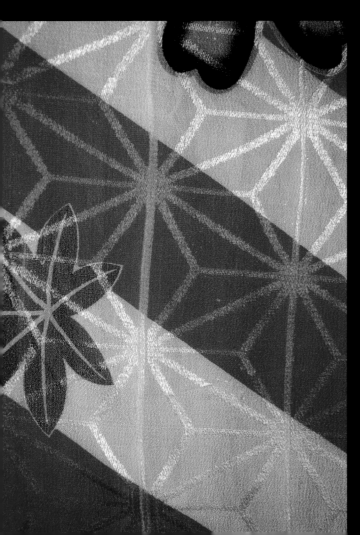

Ladies kimono lining (*juban)* remnant. Silk dyed print. Showa Period, 14 x 7. Taken from a background detail to the forefront, the enlarged *asanoha* pattern makes a strong statement.

Ladies kimono lining *(juban)* remnant. Silk dyed print. Showa Period, 4 x 2. Elegant tassel motif on solid red ground color.

Ladies kimono lining remnant. Silk dyed print. Showa Period, 5 x 5.5. A detail of subtle color graduation on leaf.

Young girl's kimono remnant. Cotton dyed print. Showa Period, 14 x 6.5. A sweet design with a carpet of cherry blossoms, a cloud motif filled with assorted blossoms

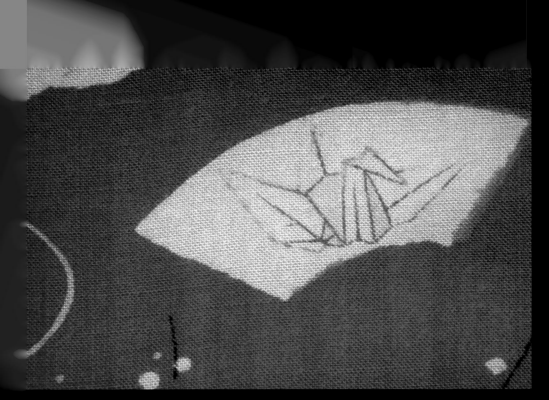

Detail of paper crane (*oritzuru*) from previous textile.

Young woman's kimono fragment. Cotton dyed print. Showa Period, 9 x 7. A paulownia motif.

Flower diamond (*hanabishi*) detail from previous textile. 3 x 2.

Paulownia detail from previous textile. 4 x 2.

Ladies kimono fragment. Silk dyed print. Showa Period, 7 x 6.5. A partition
(kicho) historically used by Japanese nobility is shown with *sayagata* detailing.

Tortoise shell hexagons (*kikko*), plum blossoms and *kanoko* dot motifs. 7 x 6.5. Remnant from previous textile.

Young woman's kimono fragment. Silk with damask effect. Showa Period, 7 x 6.5. Blossoms and green shoots.

Girl's kimono remnant. Silk dyed print with damask effect. Showa Period, 13 x 7. A flower cart motif with an assortment of vivid blossoms.

Girl's kimono remnant. Silk dyed print with damask effect. Showa Period, 7 x 6.5. A double petal chrysanthemum with twisted petals and metallic thread detailing.

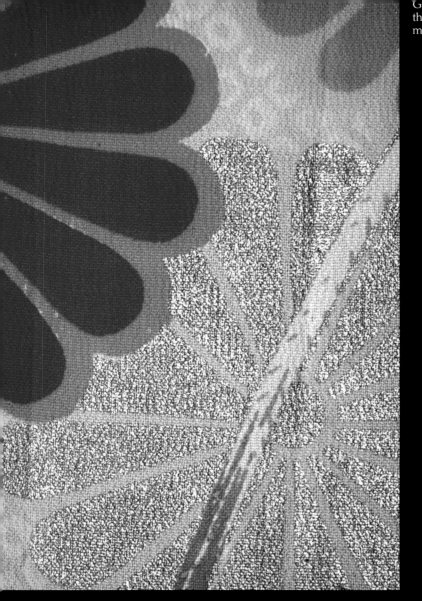

Girl's kimono fragment. Silk dyed print with metallic thread details. Showa Period, 6 x 5.5. Chrysanthemum motifs in silver, red and pink.

A brilliant red chrysanthemum on delicate *kanoko* dot background. 7 x 6.5. Remnant from previous textile.

Girl's kimono lining (*juban*) remnant. Cotton dyed print. Showa Period, 6 x 6.5. A treasure boat motif (*takarabune*) is an indication that this piece is from a New Year's kimono. The Seven Deities of Good Fortune (*Shichifukujin*) are said to come to port on New Years Eve, bringing happiness to everybody.

Detail of mast from previous textile.

An imperial palace doll is shown seated amongst plum blossoms and chrysanthemums. If you look closely at the doll's clothes, he is wearing a blue bib (*haragake*) with an *asanoha* pattern. 7 x 6.5. Remnant from previous textile.

Girl's kimono fragment. Silk dyed print. Showa Period, 7 x 7. Plum blossoms arranged in a circle complimenting the circular *temari* ball shape. One ball has a twisted plum blossom (*nejiume*) motif paired with a small *kanoko* dot design.

Detail of blossoms. Note the small spinning top on the white square. 7 x 7. Remnant from previous textile.

Girl's kimono fragment. Cotton dyed print. Showa
Period, 7 x 4.5. Cloud with *temari* design.

Cord and *temari* detail. 5 x 4.5. Remnant from previous textile.

Young girl's kimono remnant. Silk dyed print with damask effect. Showa Period, 8 x 6. A *temari* with a lush floral design including peonies, cherry blossoms and semicircular waves. The colorful threads on *temari* are symbolic, wishing the recipient a brilliant and happy life.

Girl's kimono fragment. Silk dyed print. Showa Period, 8 x 6. A double petal chrysanthemum in white and orange.

Girl's kimono fragment. Silk dyed print. Showa Period, 7 x 6.5.
Multi layers of petals add depth to this simple white chrysanthemum.
Crease due to age.

Young girl's kimono fragment. Silk dyed print. Showa Period, 6 x 7.5. A flying crane motif (5.5").

Detail of crane from previous kimono. 7 x 7.5.

Woman's kimono lining (*juban*) remnant. Synthetic dyed print. Heisei Period, 6 x 5. A simple check.

Woman's kimono remnant. Synthetic dyed print. Heisei Period, 6 x 5. Flowers and foliage.

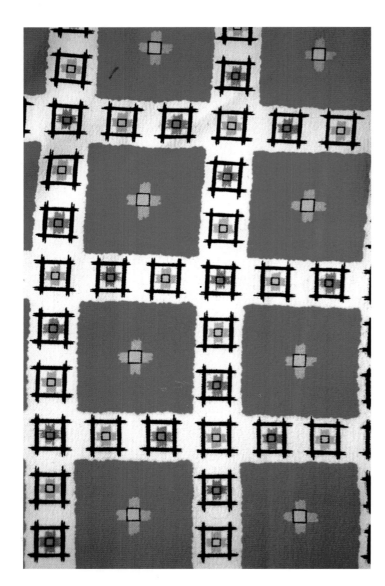

Woman's kimono remnant. Synthetic dyed print. Showa Period, 6 x 5. A *Kasuri* like design.

Woman's kimono fragment. Cotton dyed print. Heisei Period, 14 x 7.5. A stylized phoenix and lattice design.

Chapter Three
Maple Leaves

Woman's kimono remnant. Silk dyed print with damask effect. Showa Period, 14 x 7.5. A fan motif embellished with bamboo and *kanoko* dot motifs.

Detail of bamboo from previous textile. 4 x 2.5.

Woman's kimono lining (*juban*) fragment. Silk dyed print. Showa Period, 4 x 5. A bamboo silhouette.

Girl's kimono fragment. Silk dyed print. Showa Period, 11 x 6.5.

Woman's kimono lining (*juban*) fragment. Silk dyed print. Showa Period, 7 x 6.5. A maple leaf and a small *kanoko* design.

Girl's kimono remnant. Cotton dyed print. Showa Period, 11 x 6.5. An orange cloud with blossoms.

85

Woman's kimono lining (*juban*) remnant. Silk dyed print.
Showa Period, 14 x 6.5. *Kanoko* dot pattern.

Woman's kimono lining (*juban*) remnant. Silk dyed print. Showa Period, 14 x 6.5. One woven-like block motif on solid red ground color.

Woman's kimono remnant. Silk dyed print with damask effect. Showa Period, 4 x 3. *Kanoko* dot and petal design.

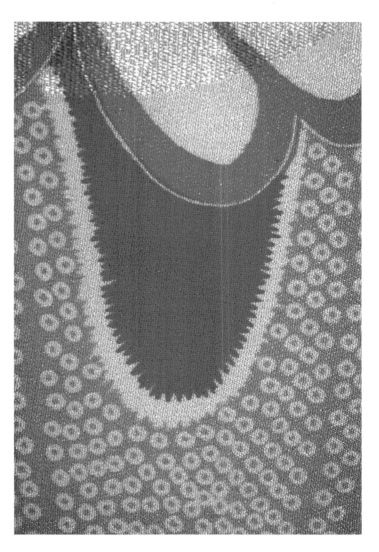

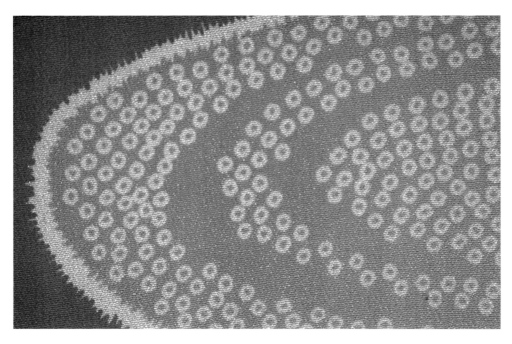

Woman's kimono remnant. Silk dyed print. Showa Period, 4 x 3.5. Overall *kanoko* dot design in a petal.

Woman's kimono lining (*juban*) remnant. Silk dyed print. Showa Period, 14 x 6.5. A beautiful diamond lattice (*tasuki*) pattern. *Discoloring due to age.*

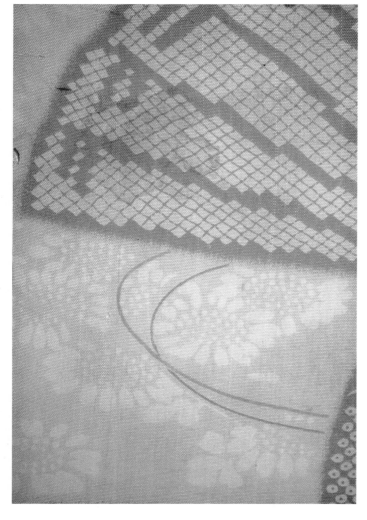

Woman's kimono remnant. Silk dyed print. Showa Period, 7 x 6.5. Fan with *a kanoko* dot pattern. *Discoloring due to age.*

Detail of maple leaf from previous textile. 3 x 2.

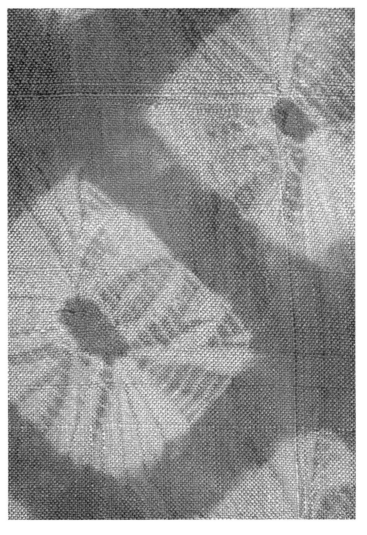

Woman's kimono lining (*juban*) remnant.
Silk *shibori* print. Showa Period, 4 x 3.5.

Woman's kimono remnant. Silk dyed print. Showa Period, 12 x 6.5. Small fans, pine tree and plum blossom motifs. The shape of the fans is echoed by the larger orange and cream triangular blocks.

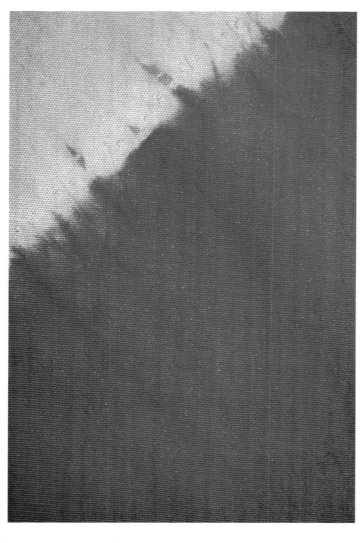

Woman's kimono lining (*juban*) remnant. Silk *shibori* dyed print. Showa Period, 14 x 6.5.

Woman's kimono remnant. Silk
dyed print. Showa Period, 6 x 5.
A bamboo motif.

Woman's kimono remnant. Silk dyed print. Showa Period, 6 x 6.5. Chrysanthemums and diamond motifs.

Girl's kimono remnant. Silk dyed print with damask effect. Showa Period, 7 x 6.5. A kaleidoscope of blossoms.

Chrysanthemums and plum blossoms. 7 x 6.5. Remnant from previous kimono.

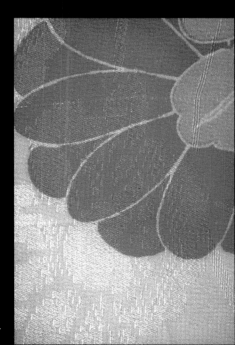

Girl's kimono remnant. Silk dyed print with damask. Showa Period, 4 x 3. Chrysanthemum petals.

Woman's kimono remnant. Silk dyed print.
Showa Period, 3 x 2.5. Petals and a *seyagata*
pattern on orange ground color. The following
two pictures are from this kimono.

Girl's kimono remnant. Silk dyed print with
damask effect. Showa Period, 3 x 2.5. An
orange chrysanthemum motif.

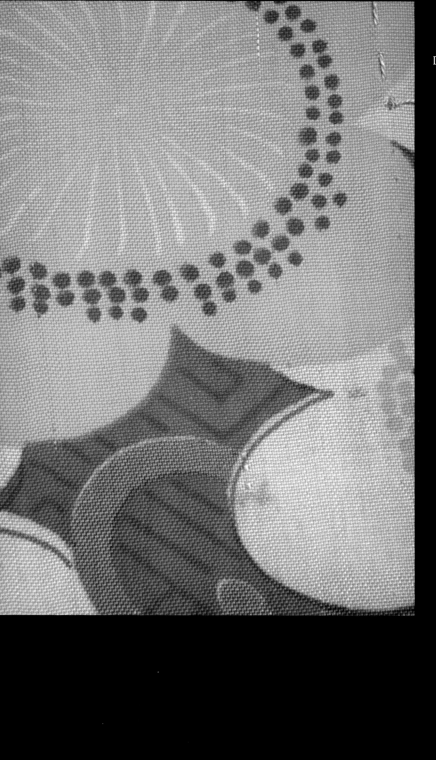

Detail of petals of yellow blossom. 4 x 3.

Outline of blossom. 3 x 2.5.

Detail of diamond shaped flowers in a hexagon *(kikko-hanabishi)* on a fan motif. Note the subtle shifts in color on the fan to delineate the folds. 4 x 6.5. Remnant from previous textile.

Detail of the lid to the *kaioke*. 5 x 7. Remnant from previous textile.

Woman's kimono remnant. Silk dyed print with damask effect.
Showa Period, 9 x 7. A gorgeous hexagonal container (*kaioke*)
used to store clam shells. The shells are used in the ancient shell
matching game *kaiawase*. The container is decorated with semicircular waves, bamboo leaves, ginko blossoms and a large blue
cloud. The cloud itself is made up of a tiny *kanoko* dot design. The
background of the fabric features a curvy hourglass design with a
chrysanthemum. This design is referred to as *kiku-tatewaku*.

Woman's kimono remnant. Silk crepe dyed print with metallic details. Showa Period, 0 x 6.5. A large crest design featuring butterflies and blossoms.

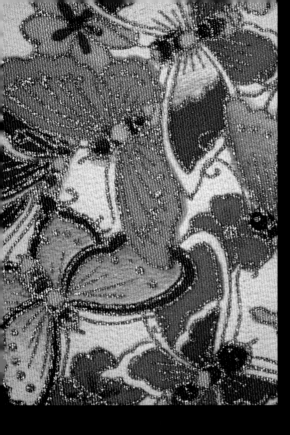

Detail of butterflies from previous textile. 3 x 2.5.

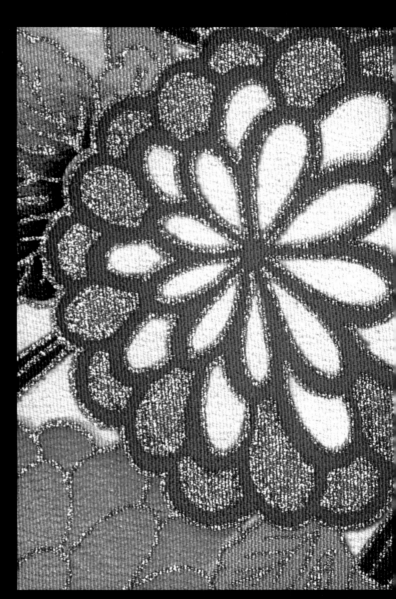

Detail of chrysanthemum from previous textile. 4 x 2.

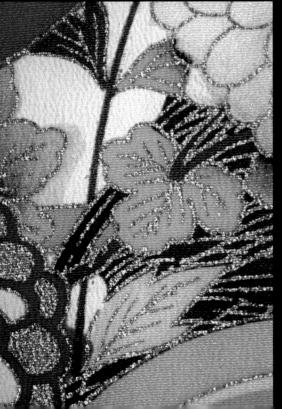

Detail of blossoms from previous kimono. 4 x 2.

Woman's kimono remnant. Silk dyed print with damask effect. Showa Period, 7 x 6.5. Blossoms and leaves on a *seyagata* background.

Subtle fan motifs. 7 x 6.5. Remnant from previous textile.

Young girl's kimono remnant. Silk dyed print. Showa Period, 4 x 5. Cluster of plum blossoms. The following two pictures are from the same kimono.

A pinwheel motif.

A *temari* ball.

Young girl's kimono remnant. Silk dyed print. Showa Period, 6 x 5. Paper crane (*oritzuru*) motif with *kanoko* dots.

Chrysanthemums and a paper crane with small crest details on wings. Remnant from previous textile.

Young girl's kimono remnant. Silk crepe (*kinsha*) dyed print. Showa Period, 6.5 x 5. A flying crane motif. *Discoloring due to age.*

Ladies kimono fragment. Silk dyed print. Showa Period, 8 x 6.5. An elegant pattern
of pine tree motifs and plum blossoms.

Woman's kimono fragment. Silk dyed print. Showa Period, 7 x
6.5. Scattered maple leaves and pine trees.

Plum blossoms and two buildings with thatched roofs. A lattice of
tortoise shell hexagons (*kikko*) forms the roof of one. 7 x 6.5. Remnant from previous textile.

Boy's kimono lining (*juban*) fragment. Rayon (*jinken*) dyed print. Showa Period, 11 x 5.5. A pine tree branch and a samurai helmet (*kabuto*). *Discoloring due to age.*

Detail of the samurai helmet from previous remnant.

Woman's kimono fragment. Silk crepe (*kinsha*) dyed print with metallic detailing. Showa Period, 7 x 7. Blossoms and foliage.

Blossoms. 6.5 x 7. Remnant from previous textile.

Woman's kimono remnant. Silk dyed print. Showa Period, 13 x 7. Naturalistic design of
wild flowers on solid cream ground color.

Detail from previous textile.

Detail of the band from previous textile.

Woman's kimono remnant. Silk dyed print. Showa Period, 14 x 7. A diamond lattice
pattern with maple leaves, plum blossoms and bamboo shoots.

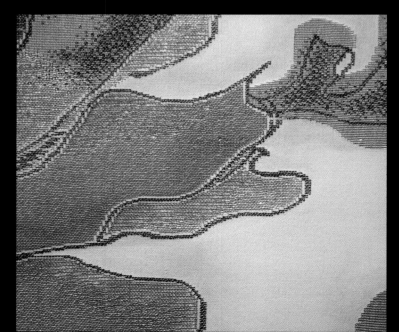

Woman's obi fragment. Silk
woven with metallic threads.
Showa Period, 7 x 5.

Woman's kimono fragment. Silk crepe dyed print. Showa
Period, 7 x 6.5. Blossoms and bamboo motifs.

Vines and bamboo from previous kimono textile. 7 x 6.5.

Woman's kimono fabric. Silk dyed print. Showa
Period, 9 x 7. A tranquil pattern of pine trees,
plum blossoms and a meandering stream.

Detail of pine tree motifs from previous textile. 5 x 7.

Woman's kimono remnant. Synthetic, dyed print. Showa Period, 14 x 7. Clouds and blossom motifs.

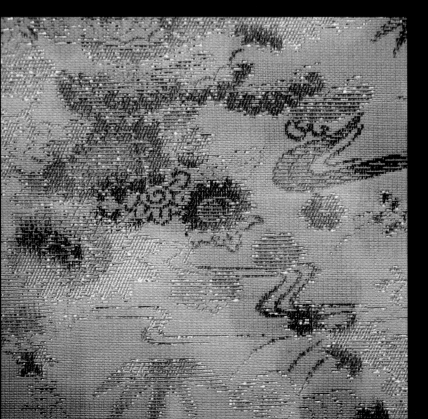

Woman's obi fragment. Silk with metallic threads, woven. Showa Period, 6 x 7. Blossoms and a stream.

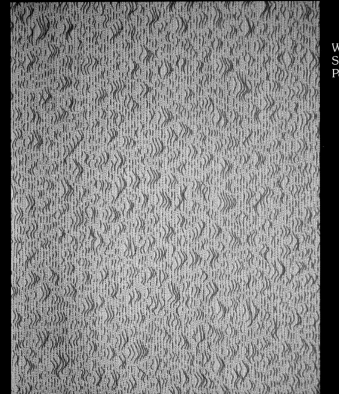

Woman's kimono remnant. Synthetic dyed print. Showa Period, 6 x 7.

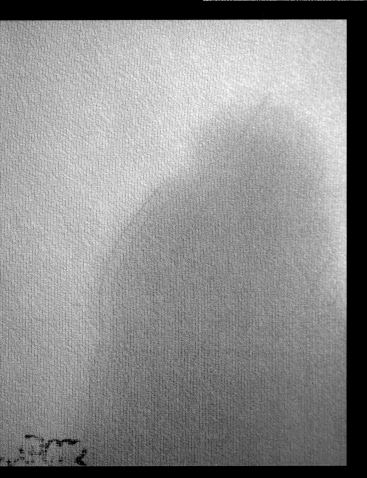

Woman's kimono remnant. Silk crepe (*kinsha*) dyed print. Showa Period, 7 x 6.5. A small black stenciled chrysanthemum in the bottom left hand corner.

Detail of cloud pattern from previous textile.

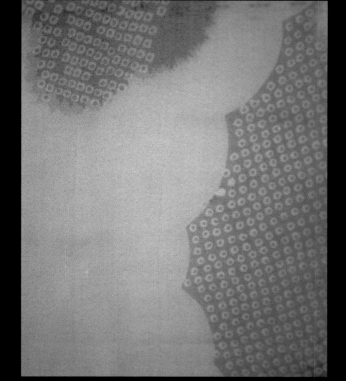

Woman's kimono lining (*juban*) remnant. Silk dyed print. Showa Period, 14 x 7 A small *kanoko* dot pattern

Woman's kimono fragment. Silk dyed print. Showa Period, 14 x 7. Leaf motifs

Woman's kimono remnant. Silk *shibori* dyed print.
Showa Period, 7 x 6.5.

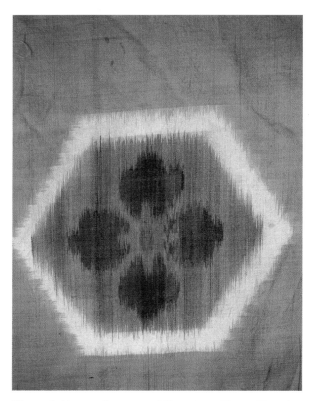

Woman's kimono fragment. Silk *meisen*. Showa Period,
7 x 6.5. Hexagonal crest with plum blossom.

Woman's kimono remnant. Silk dyed print with
damask effect. Showa Period, 14 x 6.5. print.
Bold bamboo motifs.

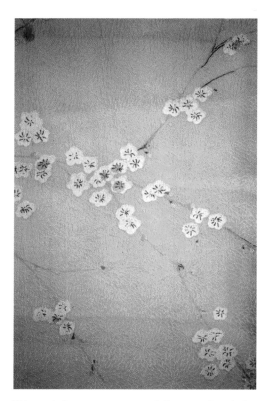

Woman's kimono remnant. Silk crepe (*kinsha*)
dyed print. Heisei Period, 14 x 6.5. A small
plum blossom design.

Chapter Four
Wisteria

Woman's kimono remnant. Silk dyed print. Showa Period, 7 x 6.5. Maples leaves and cloud motifs.

Peony, small chrysanthemum motifs and a semicircular wave pattern at the top of print. 7 x 6.5. Remnant from previous kimono.

Woman's kimono remnant. Silk crepe *(kinsha)* dyed, Showa Period, 7 x 6.5. A dramatic pink peony motif with smaller blossoms. The following three pictures are from this kimono.

A lush design with peonies and wisteria.

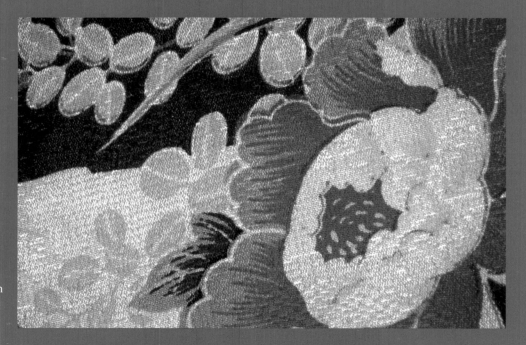

Detail of bloom from previous textile.

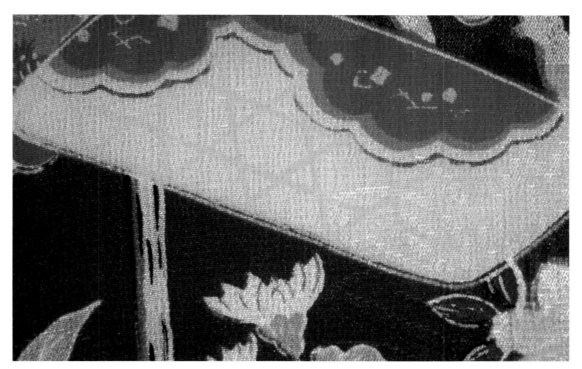

Star pattern. 4 x 2.

Woman's kimono fragment. Silk dyed print with damask effect. Showa Period, 7 x 6.5. Peony motifs and subtle *kanoko* design on petals of the lower peony.

Fan and peonies from previous textile. 9 x 6.5.

Woman's kimono fragment. Silk *meisen* print. Showa Period, 7 x
6.5. Roses and snow crystals (*yukiwa*) on a rich plum ground color.

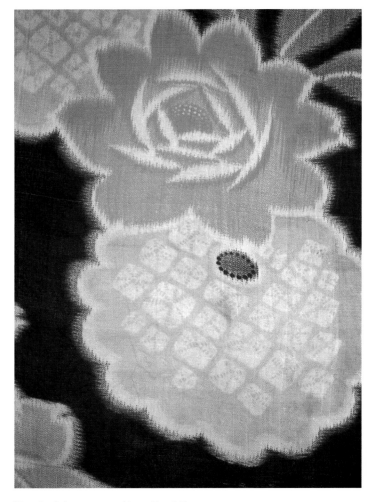

Detail of the snow *yukiwa*. 7 x 6.5.
Remnant from previous textile.

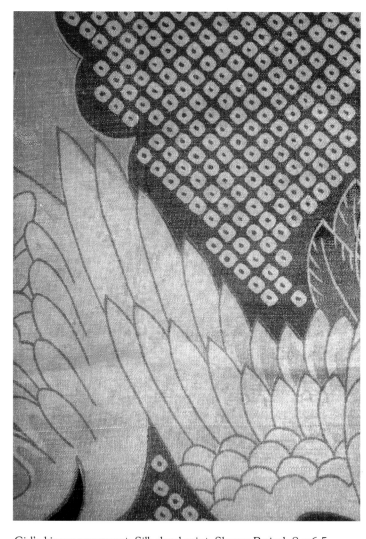

Girl's kimono remnant. Silk dyed print. Showa Period, 8 x 6.5.
Crane feathers and *kanoko* pattern on silk.

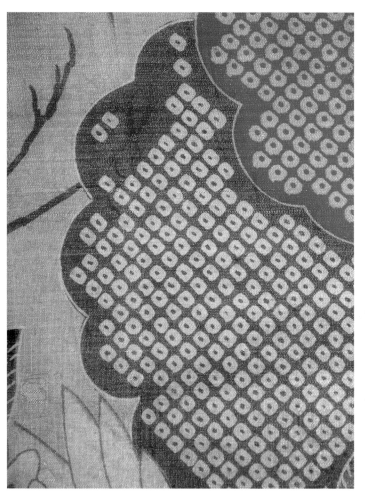

Clouds with *kanoko* pattern from previous textile. 5 x 6.5.

Young woman's kimono remnant. Silk dyed print. Showa Period, 9 x 6.5. Pine trees, waves and a small boat in a central medallion. Plum blossoms surround the tranquil scene. *Discoloring and line due to age.

Detail of a boat and blossoms from previous textile. *Discoloring due to age.

Woman's kimono fragment. Silks dyed, print. Showa Period, 14 x 6.5.
An elegant pattern featuring a flower cart/vase motif.

Detail of flower cart/vase from previous textile

Woman's kimono remnant. Silk dyed print. Showa Period, 14 x 6.5. A sweeping design of peonies, chrysanthemums, maple leaves, waves and pine trees.

Detail of blossoms from previous kimono. 6 x 4.

Detail of pine and bamboo motifs from previous kimono remnant. 5 x 4.

Blossoms and a thatched building design on fan motif from previous textile. 6 x 12.

Woman's kimono remnant. Silk dyed print with damask effect. Showa Period, 26 x 12. A lush design of fans embellished with blossoms.

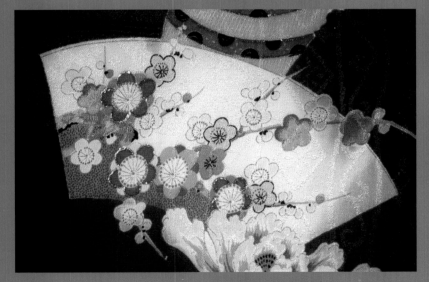

Detail of chrysanthemums and stripes from previous textile. 6 x 12.

Detail of cherry blossom fan from previous kimono. 5 x 12. A lattice with a diamond and arabesque pattern is a subtle detail on the background of the fan.

Woman's kimono remnant. Silk dyed print with damask. Showa Period, 14 x 6.5. A beautiful rich plum colored silk is set off by the stark white blossoms.

Woman's kimono remnant . Silk dyed print with damask effect. Showa Period, 14 x 6.5. Fan with scalloped edges, flowers and metallic thread detailing. *Crease line due to age.*

Detail of blossoms from previous textile.

Woman's kimono remnant. Silk dyed print. Showa Period, 14 x 6.5. Blossoms, bamboo and pine tree motifs. *Discoloring and lines are due to age.*

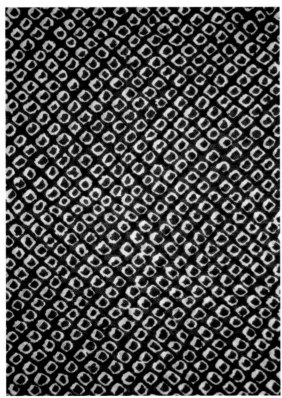

Woman's kimono fragment. Silk dyed print. Showa Period, 14 x 6.5. A delicate design of silvery-white pine trees.

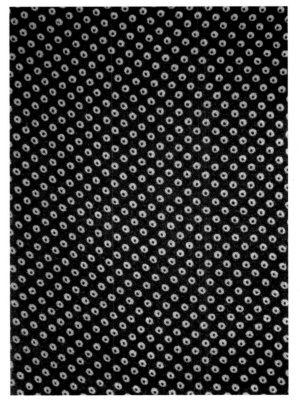

Woman's kimono lining (*juban*) remnant. Silk *kanoko shibori* print. Showa Period, 14 x 6.5.

125

Woman's kimono lining (*juban*). Silk dyed print. Showa Period, 14 x 6.5. A *kanoko* dot pattern.

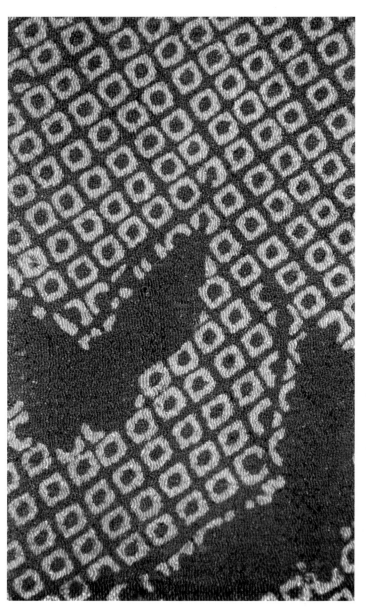

Woman's kimono remnant. Silk dyed print. Showa Period, 4 x 3.A *Kanoko* dot design.

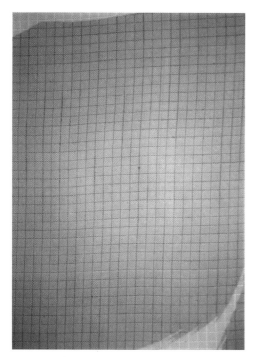

Remnant from same kimono as previous. 4 x 3. Two butterfly silhouettes on *kanoko* dot background.

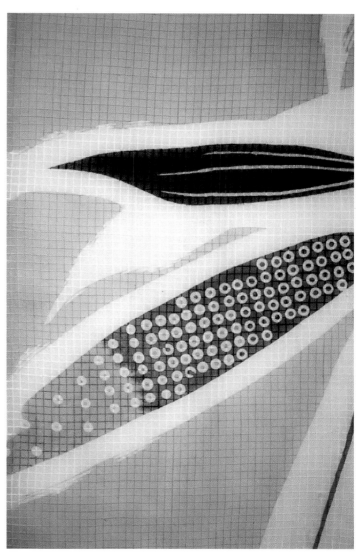

Woman's *yukata* remnant. Cotton dyed print. Showa Period, 5 x 6.5. A fine-checked pattern.

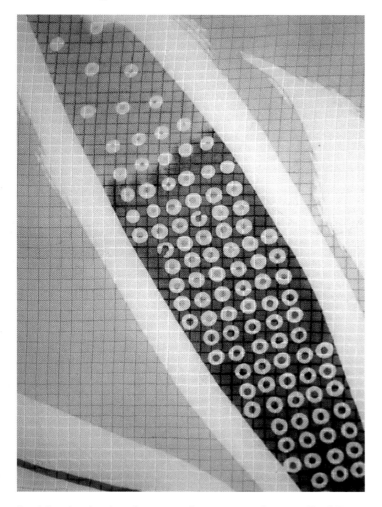

Leaf detail with *a kanoko* pattern from previous kimono. 7 x 6.5.

Detail of plum blossom crest from previous textile.

Woman's kimono remnant. Silk *meisen* design. Showa Period, 6 x 5.5. Plum blossom in a partial diamond crest.

Woman's kimono remnant. Silk *shibori* design. Showa Period, 7 x 6.5.

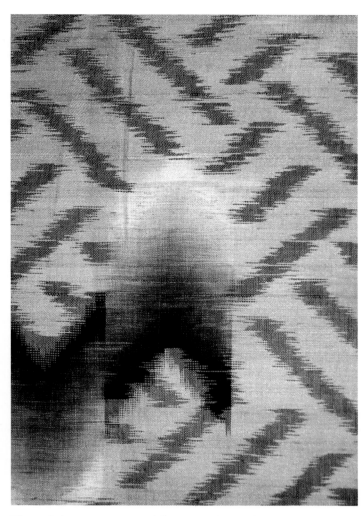

Woman's kimono remnant. Silk *meisen* design. Showa Period, 7 x 6.5. An arrow feather *(yabane)* motif.

Woman's kimono remnant. Silk *meisen* print. Showa Period, 7 x 6.5. An arrow feather *(yabane)* motif. The traditional arrow feather motif first popular in the early 17th century here modernized by the scale of its design.

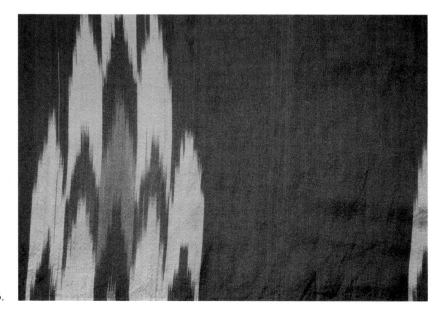

Yabane motif from previous remnant. 7 x 6.5.

Kimono remnant. Silk dyed print. Showa Period, 7 x 6.5. Fragmented bands.

Remnant from same kimono as previous. 7 x 6.5. A fragmented band. *Discoloring due to age.

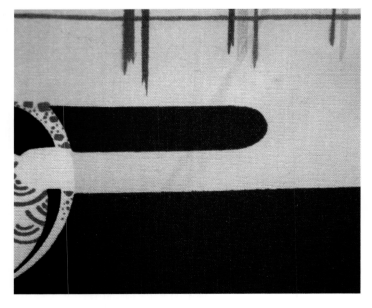

Boy's kimono remnant. Silk dyed print. Showa Period, 6 x 6. Partial crest motif visible with semicircular wave motif.

Tomoe motif. 7 x 6. Remnant from previous textile.

Woman's kimono remnant. Cotton woven design. Showa Period, 7 x 7. Semicircular waves and persimmons.

Fan, wheel, peony and other assorted floral motifs. 7 x 7. Remnant from previous textile.

Woman's kimono remnant. Cotton woven print. Showa Period, 14 x 7. A subtle pinstripe and leaves.

Woman's kimono remnant. Silk dyed print. Showa Period, 14 x 7. A checkerboard design (*ichimatsu*) with a twisted plum motif.

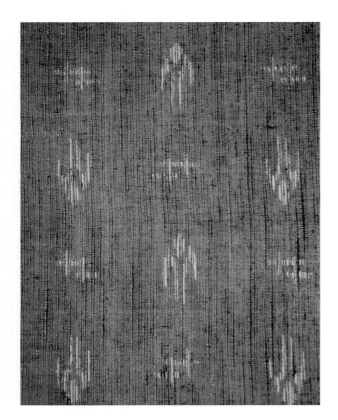

Woman's kimono remnant. Silk woven design. Showa Period, 9 x 6.5. Small bird and *ikat* in columnar design.

Woman's kimono fragment, Silk dyed print with damask effect. Heisei Period, 14 x 7. Blossoms in squares.

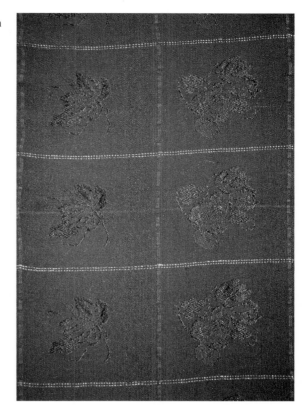

Woman's kimono remnant. Synthetic dyed print. Showa Period, 5.5 x 4. Striped pattern in three shades of purple.

Woman's kimono remnant. Silk blend dyed print. Showa Period, 5 x 4.5. A lattice pattern.

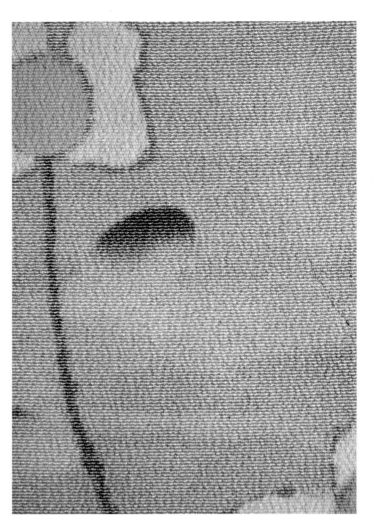

Woman's kimono remnant. Silk blend dyed print. Showa Period, 7 x 5. Dyed. Grass motif.

Woman's kimono remnant. Silk crepe (*kinsha*) dyed print. Showa Period, 4 x 3.5. A simple flower motif.

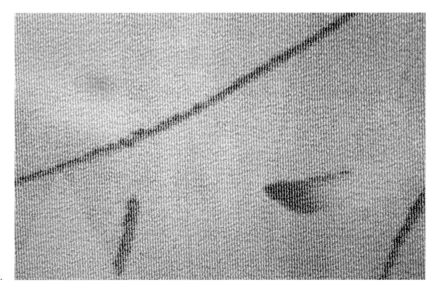

Stem from same kimono as previous. 4 x 3.5.

Woman's kimono remnant. Silk dyed print. Showa Period, 14 x 6.5. A large white peony motif. *Discoloring and lines due to age.* The following three pictures are from this kimono.

Detail of peony.

Detail of leaves.

Detail of blossoms.

Woman's kimono lining (*juban*) remnant. Silk dyed print. Showa Period, 7 x 6.

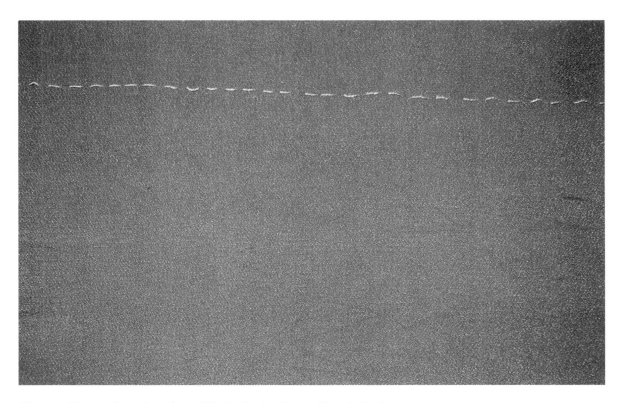

Woman's kimono (*juban*) remnant. Silk dyed print. Showa Period, 7 x 6.

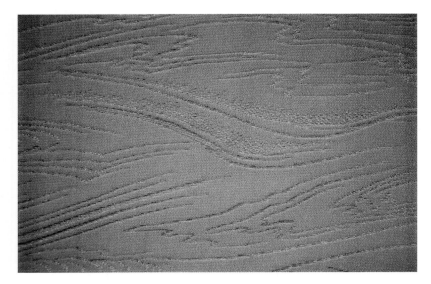

Woman's *iromuji* kimono remnant. Silk
dyed print. Showa Period, 7 x 6.

Woman's kimono lining (*juban*) remnant.
Silk dyed print. Showa Period, 14 x 7.

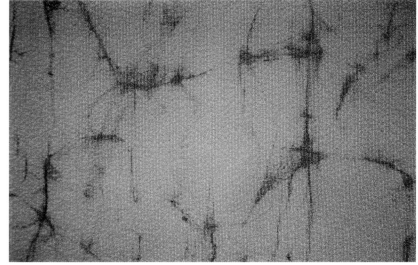

Woman's *iromuji* kimono remnant. Silk dyed print
with damask effect. Showa Period, 14 x 7. A leaf
and a small *kanoko* dot pattern.

Woman's kimono lining (*juban*) remnant. Silk dyed print with damask effect. Showa Period, 14 x 6.5. Blossoms with a subtle *kanoko* pattern.

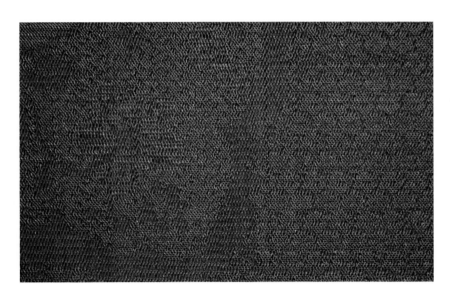

Woman's *iromuji* kimono remnant. Silk dyed print. Showa Period, 4 x 4. A small *kanoko* dot design and a plum blossom motif.

Woman's *iromuji* kimono remnant. Silk dyed print. Showa Period, 14 x 7.

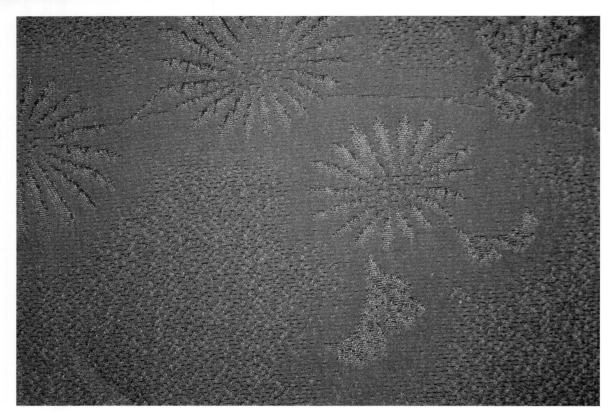

Woman's *iromuji* kimono remnant. Silk dyed print with damask effect. Showa Period, 14 x 7. Chrysanthemum motifs.

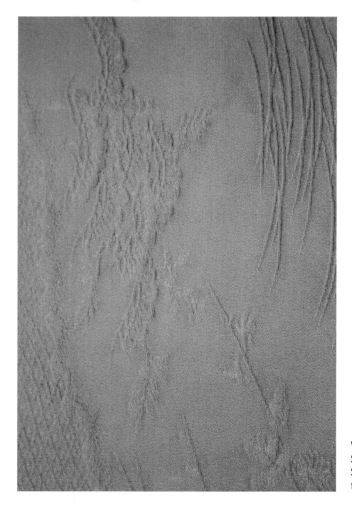

Woman's *iromuji* kimono remnant. Silk crepe (*kinsha)* dyed print. Showa Period, 14 x 7. A raised pattern of pine trees and mountains.

Chapter Five
Bamboo Shoots

Woman's kimono remnant. Silk blend dyed print. Showa Period, 14 x 7. A scalloped medallion with bamboo motifs. *Discoloring due to age.* The following six remnants are all from this same kimono.

A scalloped medallion with peony blossoms.

Vines and scalloped medallion with blossoms. 6 x 13.

A scalloped medallion with leaves. 7 x 4.

A scalloped medallion with chrysanthemums. 13 x 6.5.

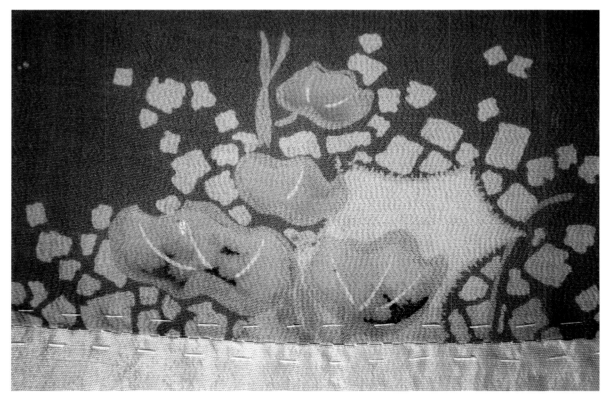

Blossoms. 13 x 5.

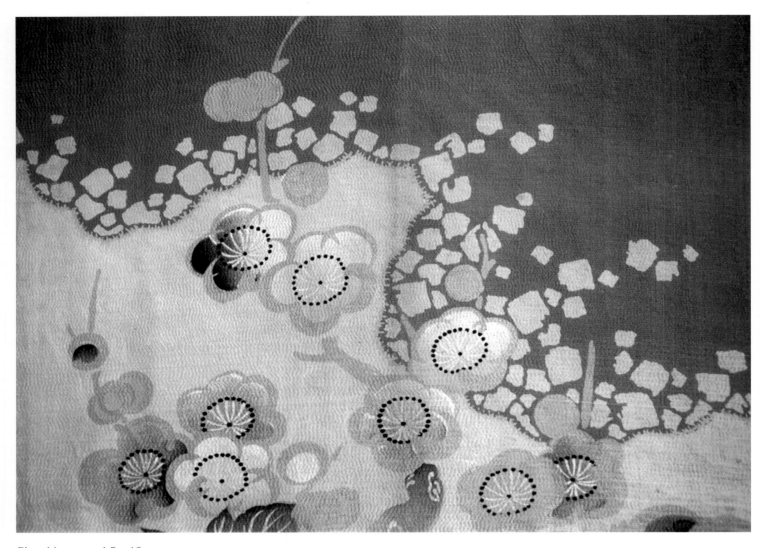

Plum blossoms. 4.5 x 13.

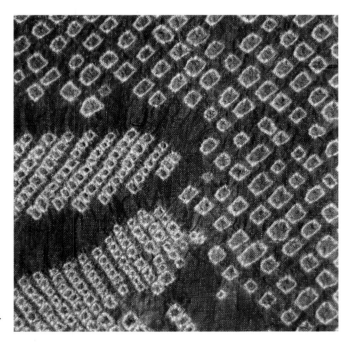

Cotton *kanoko shibori* remnant.
Showa Period, 6 x 5.5.

Silk *shibori* obi remnant,
Showa Period, 14 x 7.

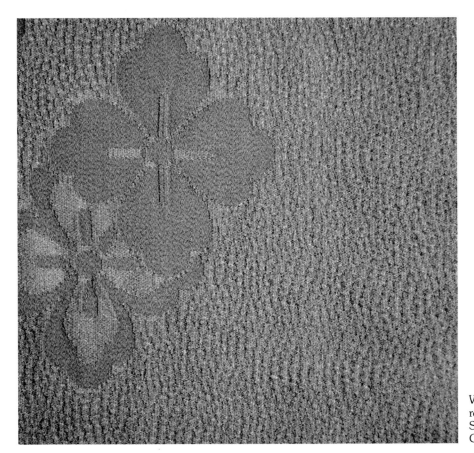

Woman's *iromuji* kimono
remnant. Silk dyed print.
Showa Period, 6 x 5.5.
Cherry blossom crests.

Woman's kimono remnant. Silk dyed print with damask effect. Showa Period,
7 x 6.5. Cherry blossoms on *asanoha* patterned background.

Detail of blossoms and background
from previous textile. 6 x 5.5.

Woman's kimono remnant. Silk *meisen* design. Showa
Period, 14 x 7. A persimmon on a vine.

Woman's *iromuji* kimono remnant. Silk
dyed print. Showa Period, 14 x 7.

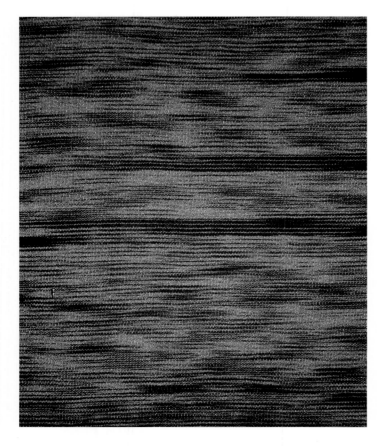

Woman's kimono remnant. Silk dyed print. Showa Period, 14 x 7. Striking black and green design.

Woman's kimono remnant. Synthetic dyed print. Showa Period, 14 x 7. Stripes.

Woman's kimono fragment. Cotton woven design. Showa Period, 14 x 7.

Woman's kimono remnant.
Synthetic dyed print. Heisei
Period, 6 x 5.5. Metallic
gold plum blossoms.

Woman's kimono remnant. Synthetic dyed print. Heisei Period, 7 x 6.5.
Chrysanthemums, fan with *kanoko* dot design and maple leaf motifs.

Chapter Six
Waves

Detail of Japanese hand drum (*tsuzumi*)a Japanese flute (*shakuha-chi*) and fan. Small flower diamonds (*hanabishi*) adorn the drum.

Boy's kimono remnant. Rayon (*jinken*) dyed print. Showa Period, 20x 13. A playful design with a turtle, flying cranes, shells and masts. The masts feature a subtle semicircular wave pattern and a kanji character for *kotobki* or congratulations. The following three pictures are from this kimono.

Detail of flying cranes.

Detail of turtle and shell.

Boy's kimono remnant. Rayon (*jinken*) dyed print. Showa Period, 10 x 7. The treasure boat motif (*takarabune*) is part of an overall New Years Eve theme. There are more than seven design patterns on the boat alone, including; tortoise shell (*kikko*), wave (*seyagata*), diamond flower *(hanabishi)* and a pine tree. The kanji character on the mast reads *kotobuki* or congratulations.

Detail of toy carp from previous textile. 8 x 7.

Boy's kimono fragment. Silk dyed print. Showa Period, 9 x 7. An elaborate samurai hat (*kabuto*) with a tassel and small chrysanthemum crest.

Detail of patterns on the *kabuto* from previous textile.

Detail of *kabuto* from previous textile.

Boy's kimono remnant. Rayon (*jinken*) dyed print. Showa Period, 7 x 5. Diamond flower (*hanabishi*) motif on solid turquoise blue ground color. The following five pictures are from this kimono.

A child's kite. 4 x 3.5.

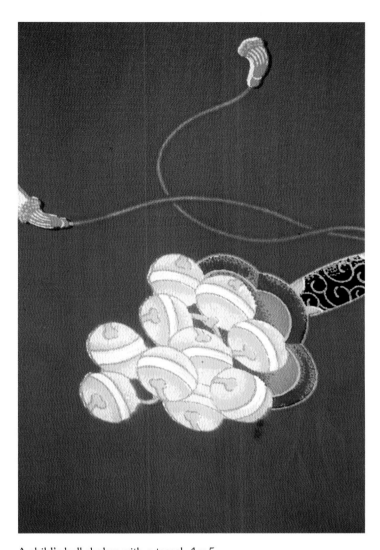

A child's bell shaker with a tassel. 4 x 5.

A banner with a mask motif. 7 x 8.

Lions mask (*shishi-gashira*) and fan. The lion dance (*shishi-mai)* is not just for entertainment but thought to ward off evil, bring good health and bountiful harvests.

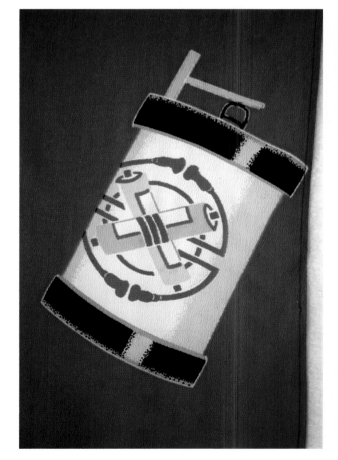

A lantern motif. 4 x 5.

Woman's kimono remnant. Silk blend, dyed print with damask effect. Showa Period, 7 x 6.5. Elegant pine tree motifs.

A colorful phoenix is surrounded by blossoms. 7 x 6.5. Remnant from previous textile.

Woman's kimono remnant. Silk dyed print. Showa Period, 14 x 7. Scattered cherry blossoms and bamboo.

Young woman's kimono remnant. Silk dyed print with damask effect. Showa Period, 14 x 7. An exquisite circular plum blossom motif.

Woman's *yukata* fragment. Cotton dyed print. Blossoms and flower bud on striped background. *Discoloring and lines due to age.*

Detail of flower buds from previous *yukata* remnant.

Young woman's kimono remnant. Silk dyed print. Showa Period, 7 x 6.5. A
Japanese iris and semicircular wave motifs. *Discoloring due to age.*

Detail of the long fluid curves of the waves, 7 x 6.5. Remnant from previous kimono.

Woman's *yukata* remnant. Cotton dyed print. Showa Period,
7 x 7. Bamboo, small dragonflies and a *tasuki* pattern.

Detail of the bamboo and *tasuki* pattern.
7 x 7. Remnant from previous textile.

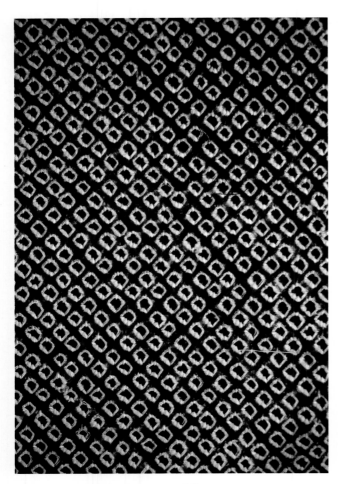

Kimono lining (*juban*) remnant. Silk
shibori print. Showa Period, 14 x 7.

Kimono lining (*juban)* remnant. Silk *kanoko
shibori* print. Showa Period, 14 x 7.

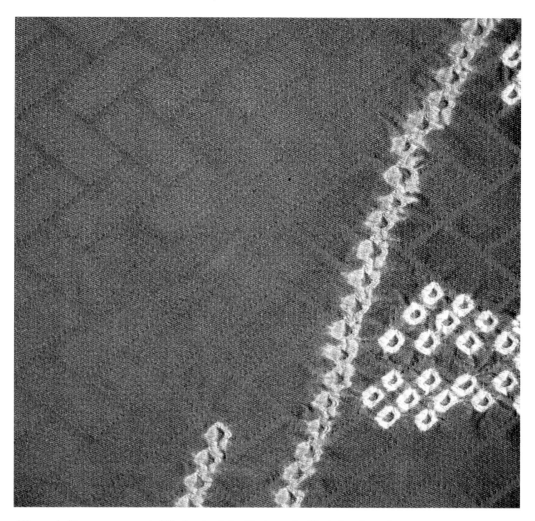

Woman's kimono remnant. Silk dyed print with damask effect. An elegant
pattern of interlocking tiles and a *kanoko* dot design. 5 x 6.

A *kasuri* striped kimono remnant,
Showa Period, 8 x 6.

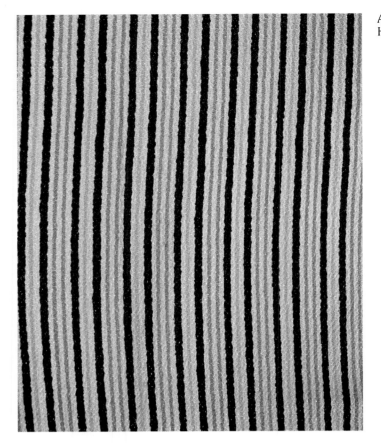

A synthetic striped remnant, dyed,
Heisei Period, 7 x 6.5.

Synthetic remnant, dyed, Heisei Period, 8 x 6. A mesh design.

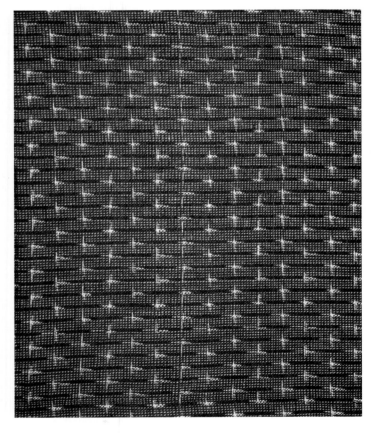

A *kasuri* remnant, woven, Showa Period, 6 x 5.5.
Cotton with a double *ikat* design.

A *kasuri* remnant, woven, Showa Period, 6 x 5.
Cotton with an elaborate wave motif.

Woman's *iromiji* kimono remnant. Silk dyed print. Showa
Period, 7 x 6.5. A fractured line design.

Woman's kimono remnant. Synthetic dyed print.
Heisei Period, 5 x 4.5. Small checked pattern.

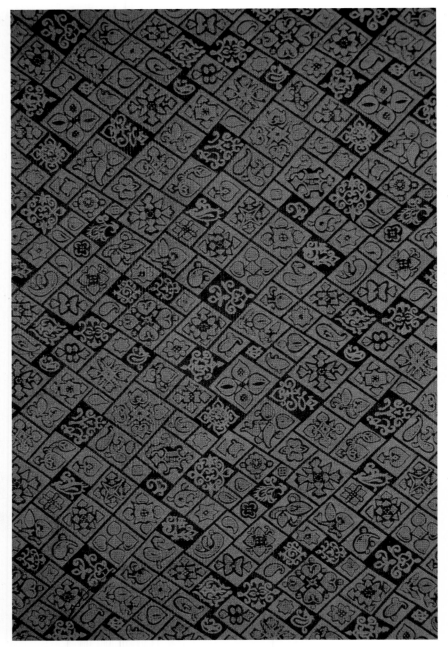

Woman's kimono remnant. Silk dyed print. Heisei Period, 6 x 5.5. A geometric step pattern.

Woman's kimono fragment. Synthetic dyed print. Heisei Period, 14 x 7. Small motifs fill a busy checked pattern.

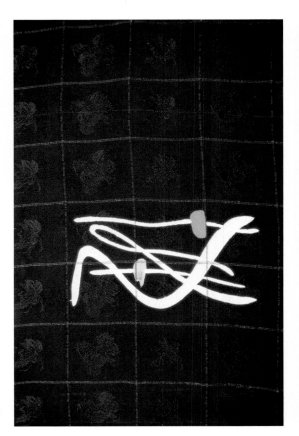

Woman's kimono remnant. Silk dyed print with damask effect. Heisei Period, 14 x 7. An abstract white swirl against a demure blossom and check background.

Woman's kimono remnant. Synthetic dyed print. Heisei Period,
6 x 5.5. Chrysanthemums.

Chapter Seven
Clouds

Woman's kimono remnant . Silk dyed print. Showa Period, 6 x 5. The image of a woman and solitary maple leaf make for an elegant piece.

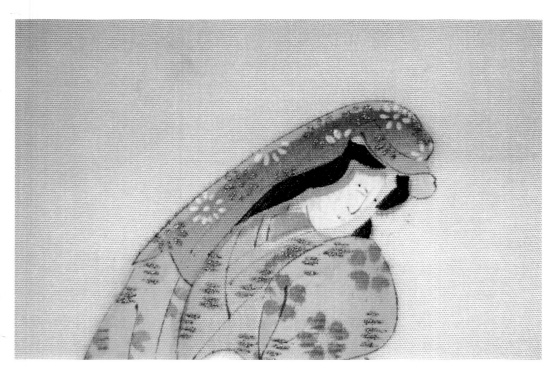

Detail of a woman from previous kimono remnant. The woman is wearing her *kosode* draped over her head. The practice of covering your head called *katsugu* in Japanese began in the Muromachi Period. (Dalby, *Kimono Fashioning Culture*, p.36)

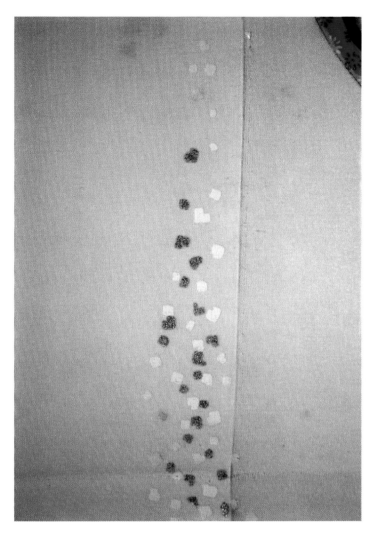

The journey of the falling leaf symbolized by the vertical arrangement small gold and white motifs. 8 x 6.5. Remnant from the previous textile.

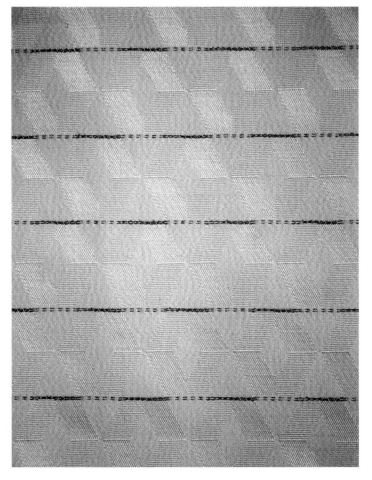

Woman's kimono remnant. Silk dyed print with damask effect. Showa Period, 14 x 7. A subtle diagonal block design with metallic thread details.

Ladies kimono fragment. Silk dyed print. Showa Period, 9 x 6.5.
A maple leaf pattern. *Discoloring and lines due to age.

Woman's kimono remnant. Silk dyed print. Showa Period,
6.5 x 5. A trio of blossoms.

Woman's kimono remnant. Silk dyed print with damask effect. Showa Period, 7 x 6.5. Solid color (*iromuji*) kimono with metallic thread details. An elegant design of pine combs and pine needles.

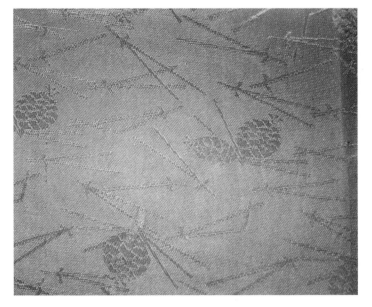

Pine combs and needles. 7 x 6.5. Remnant from previous kimono.

Woman's silk kimono remnant, dyed, Showa Period, 7 x 7. A subtle floral design in pink. *Discoloring and line due to age.*

Remnant from previous kimono. 6.5 x 7.

Woman's kimono remnant. Silk dyed print with damask effect. Showa Period, 14 x 7. Solid color (*iromuji*) kimono with subtle bamboo motif and cloud with a *kanoko* dot pattern.

Woman's kimono remnant. Silk dyed print with damask effect. Showa Period, 9 x 7. A striking chrysanthemum motif against a background of waves.

Detail of stylized waves from previous kimono remnant.

Woman's kimono remnant. Silk dyed print. Showa Period, 14 x 7. A
pictorial scene set in ancient Japan. *Crease and discoloring due to age.*
The following three pictures are from this kimono.

Detail of the women wearing *furisode* kimonos.

Detail of samurai figure and servant
by bridge and winding stream.

Detail of plum blossoms and pine trees.

Woman's woven obi fragment. Silk woven print with metallic
thread details. Heisei Period, 14 x 7.

Ladies kimono fragment. Silk crepe (kinsha) dyed print. Showa
Period, 5 x 4. Maple leaves. *Discoloring due to age.

A pink maple leaf. 5 x 4. Remnant from previous textile.
Discoloring due to age.

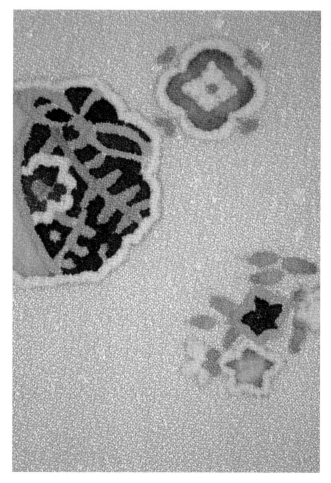

Woman's kimono remnant. Synthetic dyed print with damask effect. Showa Period, 14 x 7. A band and dot design.

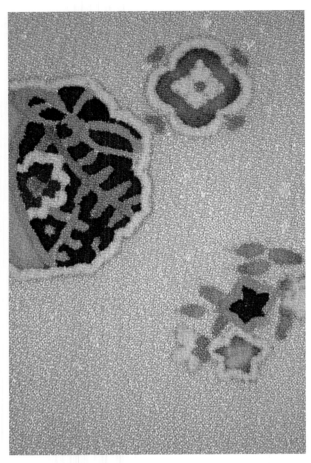

Woman's kimono remnant. Synthetic dyed print. Heisei Period, 4 x 3.5. Basket and blossom motifs.

Woman's kimono remnant. Silk dyed print with damask effect. Heisei Period, 5 x 4.5. Blossoms and stylized foliage.

Chapter Eight
Earth

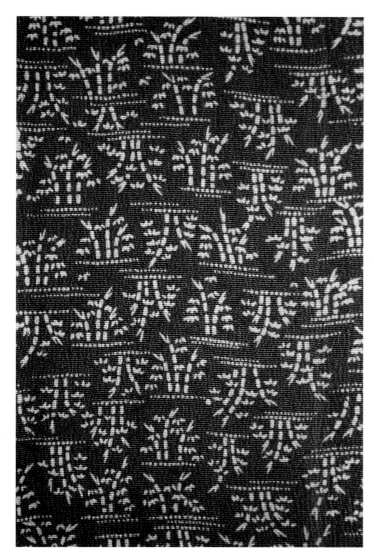

Woman's kimono remnant. Silk dyed print. Showa Period,
9 x 7. An overall pattern of bamboo shoots.

Woman's kimono lining (*juban*) remnant. Silk
kanoko shibori print. Showa Period, 5 x 4.5.

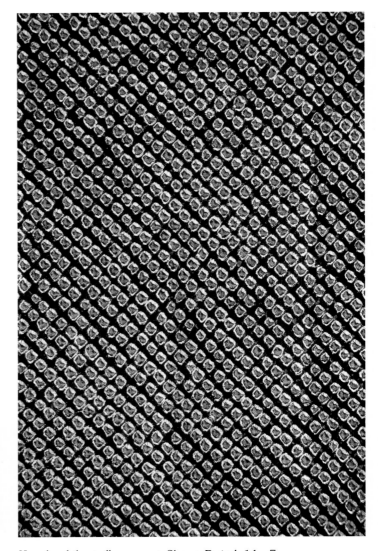

Kanoko shibori silk remnant. Showa Period, 14 x 7.

Woman's kimono remnant. Silk dyed print with damask effect. Showa Period, 9 x 6. A *kanoko* dot, chrysanthemum and lattice pattern.

Woman's *iromuji* kimono remnant. Silk dyed print. Showa Period, 14 x 7. An *asanoha* pattern with a striking white center.

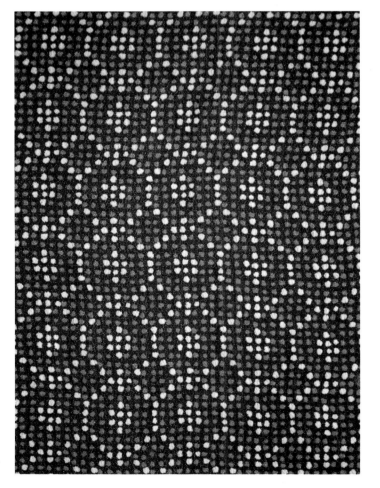

Woman's kimono remnant. Synthetic dyed print. Showa Period, 14 x 7. Overall tortoise shell *(kikko)* pattern.

Woman's kimono remnant. Silk dyed print with damask effect.
Showa Period, 7 x 7. Blossoms and leaves on a lattice background.

Detail of blossoms from same kimono as previous. 6 x 7.

Woman's kimono fragment. Silk dyed print with damask effect.
Showa Period, 4 x 3. Trio of bamboo leaves.

Woman's kimono remnant. Silk dyed print. Showa Period, 6.5 x 5.
A warped-*ikat* stripes and blossom design.

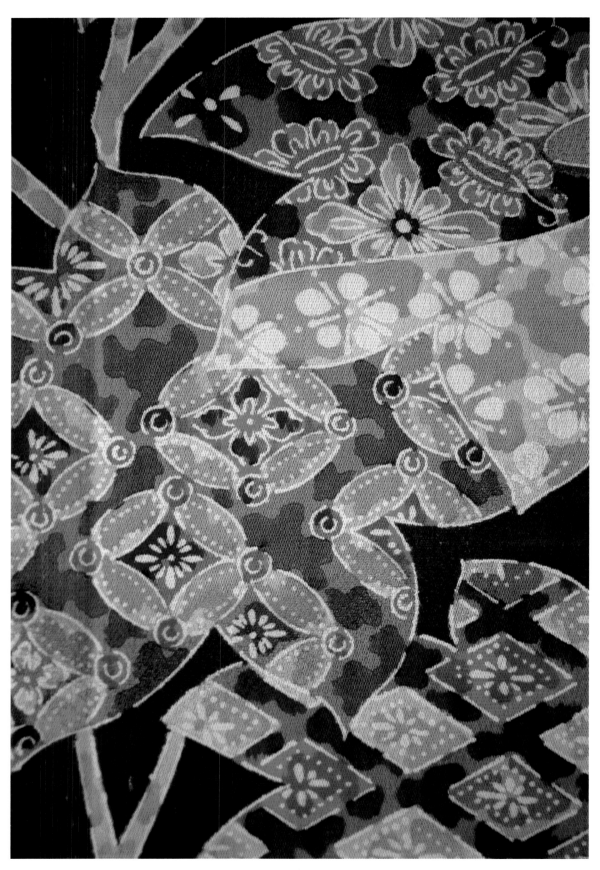

Woman's kimono fragment. Silk dyed print. Heisei Period, 10 x 7.
Ornate pattern of stylized foliage. Lattice, cherry blossom crests and
diamond flowers *(hanabishi)* are used to enhance this lavish design.

Detail of cherry blossom crest design from previous kimono remnant.

Detail of lattice and hourglass (*tatewaku*) patterns.

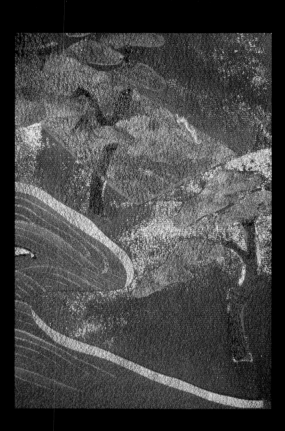

Woman's kimono remnant. Synthetic dyed print with metallic details. Showa Period, 14 x 7. Pine trees, a stream and mountain motifs.

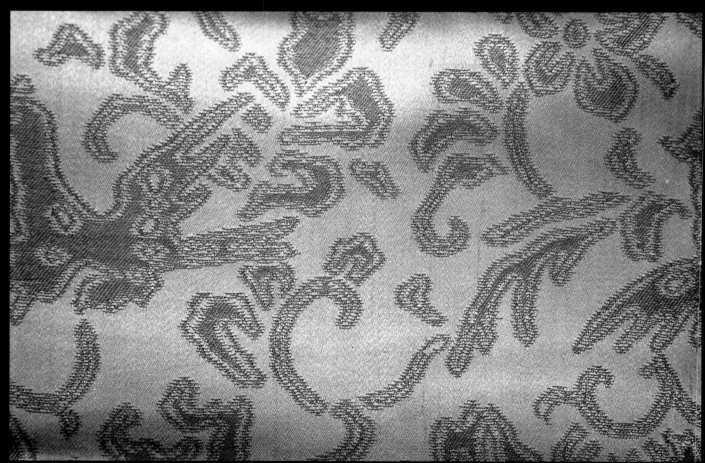

Woman's silk *obi* remnant, woven, Heisei Period, 6 x 5.5.

Woman's kimono fragment. Cotton dyed print. Showa Period, 7 x 6.5. A fan filled with assorted blossoms and a *kanoko* dot flower motif.

Peonies in burnt orange and cream. 7 x 6.5. Remnant from previous textile.

Woman's kimono remnant. Cotton dyed print. Heisei Period,
6 x 5.5. Fragmented design of semicircular waves.

Woman's silk kimono remnant,
Showa Period, 6 x 5. A columnar
pattern of organic shapes and
flowers.

Woman's silk kimono remnant with damask effect, dyed, Showa Period, 6 x 5. Hexagons, diamonds and rectangles with stylized floral motifs make for a rich pattern.

Woman's kimono remnant. Silk dyed print. Showa Period, 14 x 7. A bold striped pattern.

Woman's kimono remnant. Silk dyed print. Showa Period,
14 x 7. Fine stripes in two shades of brown.

Woman's kimono remnant. Silk dyed print. Heisei Period,
14 x 7. Undulating lines.

Woman's kimono remnant. Silk dyed print.
Heisei Period, 14 x 7. Undulating lines.

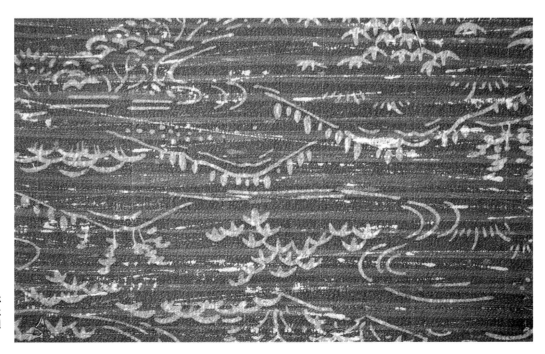

Woman's kimono remnant. Silk
dyed print. Heisei Period, 14 x
7. Subtle bamboo, stream and
mountain motifs.

Chapter Nine

Acorns

Woman's kimono lining (*juban*) remnant.
Kanoko shibori print. Showa Period, 6 x 5.

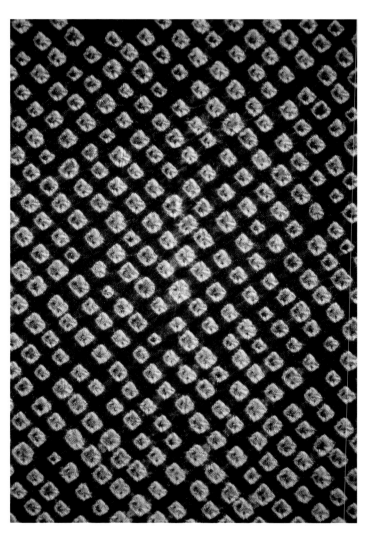

Detail of *kanoko* dot design from previous textile.

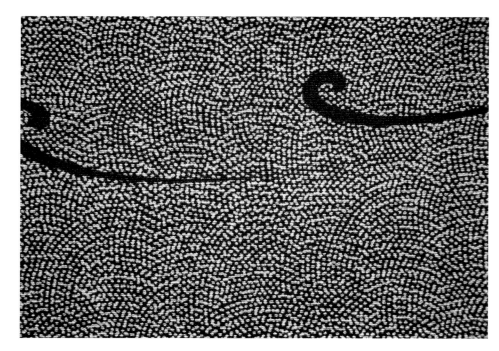

Woman's kimono remnant. Silk dyed print. Showa Period, 7 x 6.5. A semicircular wave pattern with two bold coma like motifs.

Woman's *iromuji* kimono remnant. Silk dyed print with damask effect. Heisei Period, 7 x 6.5. A solid color kimono with diamond and line motif.

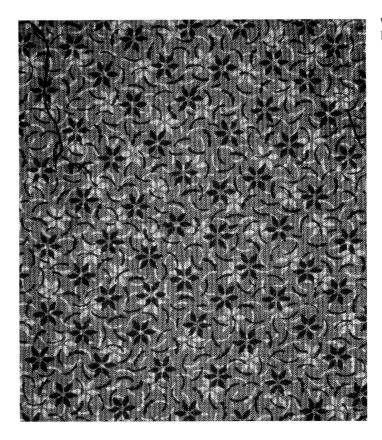

Woman's kimono remnant. Silk dyed print.
Heisei Period, 7 x 6.5. Flower and vine design.

Woman's *iromuji* kimono remnant . Silk dyed print with damask effect.
Heisei Period, 14 x 7. A cherry blossom and small dot design.

Woman's kimono lining (*juban*) remnant. Silk dyed
print. Heisei Period, 14 x 7. Solid color kimono.

Woman's *iromuji* kimono remnant. Silk with damask effect. Showa Period, 7 x 6.5. A graceful hollyhock design *Discoloring due to age.*

Woman's *iromuji* kimono remnant. Silk dyed print. Heisei Period, 7 x 6.5. Checked pattern. *Discoloring and line due to age.*

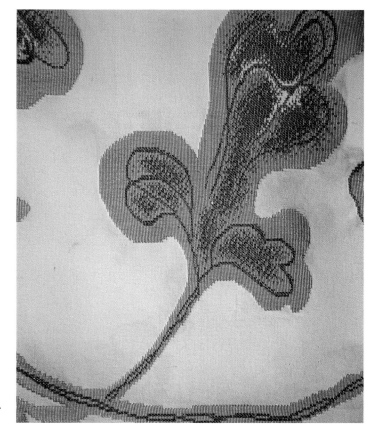

Woman's kimono remnant. Silk dyed print. Heisei Period, 14 x 7. A simple leaf motif.

Woman's *iromuji* kimono remnant. Silk dyed print. Heisei Period, 7 x 6.5. A simple blossom motif.

Woman's kimono remnant. Silk dyed print with damask effect. Showa Period, 4 x 3.5. A floral cluster.

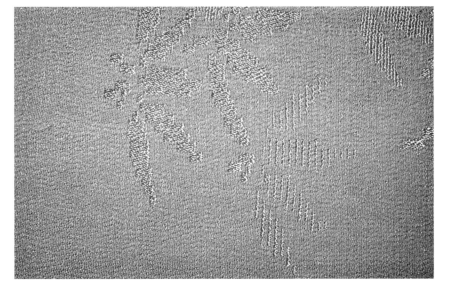

Woman's *iromuji* kimono remnant. Silk dyed print with damask *effect*. Showa Period, 14 x 7. A bamboo motif.

Woman's kimono remnant. Silk dyed print. Showa Period, 9 x 6. Maple leaves and a stream.

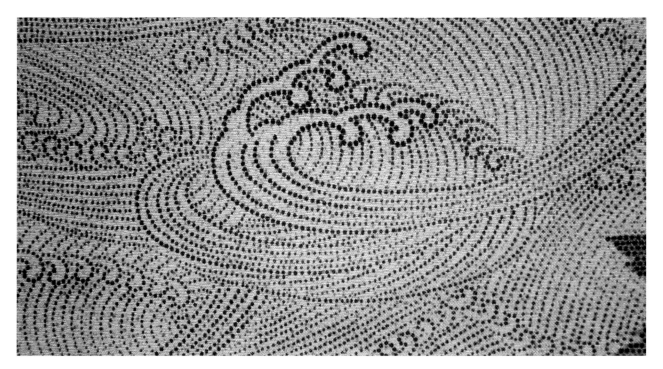

Detail of waves from previous textile. 5 x 6.

Woman's silk kimono remnant with damask effect, dyed, Showa Period, 13 x 7. A vase with peonies, chrysanthemums and assorted flowers.

Detail of tortoise shell lattice with flower (*kikko -hanabishi*) pattern. 8 x 7.

Woman's kimono remnant. Silk dyed print.
Heisei Period, 14 x 7. A mesh pattern.

Woman's kimono remnant. Silk dyed print. Heisei Period, 14 x 7. A dense lattice with diamonds.

Woman's kimono remnant. Silk dyed print.
Showa Period, 14 x 7. Radiating lines.

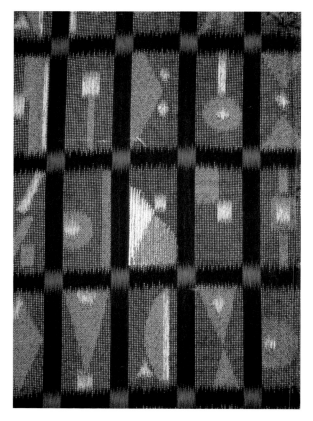

Kasuri. remnant, Showa Period, 6 x 5.5.

Kasuri remnant, dyed, Showa Period, 6 x 5.5.

Woman's kimono remnant. Silk woven design. Showa Period, 7 x 6.5. A formal design of blossoms, bamboo and chrysanthemum motifs. *Line due to age.*

Remnant from previous kimono. 6 x 6.5.

Resources

Japanese Holidays and Festivals

The falling of the cherry blossoms, the turning of the leaves and the first snow are reflected in the choice of clothing Japanese people wear. This 'sensitivity' to nature may have diminished over the centuries but there are still specific times of the years or important life events that warrant the wearing of a kimono. These special occasions for wearing the kimono include weddings, tea ceremonies, funerals, festivals and some national holidays. Below is a list of some of the major holidays in Japan. The holidays and festivals where a kimono is to be worn are explained in detail.

January 1. New Year's Day, *Oshogatsu*. This is the biggest holiday in Japan. Schools are closed for about two weeks and those hard-working salary men and women enjoy a short holiday from December 30 to January 3. It is customary to visit shrines at New Year in order to pray for prosperity and good health in the coming year. This is called *hatsu-mode*. Young ladies would don a *furisode* kimono brightly decorated. A child might have a New Year's theme kimono with traditional motifs such as spinning tops (*koma*). A married woman would wear her best *kosode*.

January 2. *Hatsu-Yume* January 2. The first dream you have after New Year's is said to be a premonition of the coming year.

Coming of Age Day (*Seijin-no-hi*) is the second Monday after New Year. When a person turns 20 in Japan he or she is considered to be legally an adult. It is customary to dress up for celebrations that include the obligatory shrine visit and then perhaps a celebration at a restaurant. A young man might wear a suit and a young lady a *furisode*.

February 2-3. *Setsubon*. Throughout Japan celebrations are held, to welcome the beginning of Spring, at temples or shrines.

March 3. Doll or Girls' Festival. *Hina matsuri*. The health and happiness of girls is prayed for on this day. Some families set up elaborate stands with dolls decked out in Heian court dress. A girl might be dressed in a special kimono and taken to the shrine to pray for her health. This tradition of displaying dolls began in the Edo Period (1603- 1868) as a way of warding off evil spirits. It is important to put the dolls away quickly after this holiday as it was believed not doing so would lessen the girl's chances of marriage.

Graduation Day. Mid- to late March. As the school year ends in April in Japan, graduation ceremonies are held during March. For female graduates of junior colleges or colleges, they may choose to wear loose pants or *hakama* over brightly colored kimonos on this special day.

April 21. Cherry Blossom Viewing. *Hanami*. Cherry blossom viewing picnics are held at picturesque parks or shrines. It is a time to gather with friends, business colleagues or family. Favored spots under flowering trees are staked out early and guarded until the entire party can arrive. A relaxed atmosphere prevails as people take in the beauty of the blossoms and enjoy the company around them.

May 3. Constitutional Memorial Day. *Kempo-kinembi*.

May 5. The first day of summer. *Rikka*.

May 5. Children's day. *Kodomo- no -hi*. On this day it is a time to pray for the welfare of all children. Originally this day was called Boys' Festival. Kites shaped like carp are flown and some homes display a samurai helmet, sword, arrows or bow.

July 7. The Star Festival. *Tanabata*.

August 7. The beginning of Autumn. *Risshu*,

Bon Festival. This is the biggest festival next to New Year. Some places in Japan celebrate this day in mid-July. The spirits of deceased family members are said to come home. During this festival a dance is held called bon *odori*. It is customary to wear a summer kimono (*yukata*)

Mid-September. Moon viewing. *Tsukimi*.

September 15. Respect For The Aged Day. *Keiro-no-hi*.

September 23 or 24. Autumnal Equinox Day. *Shubun-no-hi*.

November 15. *Shichi-go-san*. November 15 (7, 5, 3). On this day, girls and boys who are turning 3, boys aged 5 and girls aged 7 are taken to neighborhood Shinto shrines to pray for their health. Traditionally girls would wear kimonos and boys would be dressed in jackets (*haori*) and trousers (*hakama*).

December 23. The Emperor's Birthday. *Tenno-tanjobi*.

December 31. New Years Eve. *O-misoka*

Museum and Gallery Guide

Following is a list of museums in Japan, Europe, and North America that have extensive Japanese textile collections. Whether you are a serious collector, fabric designer or simply love kimonos, these inspiring and diverse museum collections are certainly a feast for the eyes. Textiles provide insight into daily life, culture and even politics. From the special exhibitions staged by the V & A to the Imperial kimonos at the Ome museum in Tokyo, museums have something for all kimono enthusiasts.

In order to plan your excursion, it is best to check with the museums online sites before setting out. Up coming exhibitions, closures and detailed access maps are all available online.

If you are researching pieces from your own collection, many of these facilities have reference libraries, microfilm, magazines, exhibition catalogues and research bulletins.

For a complete list of Japanese museums there is an online resource http://www.dnp. co.jp/museum/icc-e.html.

For the United States, go to http://www. museumsusa.org/ or see the comprehensive site http://www.icom.museum/vlmp/lists.html for worldwide locations.

Tokyo and surrounding Kanto Area
Itchiku Kubota Museum
2255 Kawaguchi, Fuji Kawaguchiko-cho Minamitsuru-gun. Yamanashi 401-0304
Website: http://www.itchiku-tsujigahana. co.jp/

Oume Kimono Museum
4-629 Baigo , Ome-shi
Tel: 0428-762019
Website: http://www3.kitanet.ne.jp/~kimono/ oume/. The site is in Japanese.
Displays clothes from the Imperial household, period dress and clothing of the former Imperial Highness Nashimoto-no-miya.

The Bunka Gakuen Costume Museum
3-22-7 Yoyogi Shibuya-ku near Bunka Women's University
Shinjuku Station, JR Keio & Odakyu lines
Tel: 03-3299-2387
Website: http://www.bunka.ac.jp/museum/ hakubutsu.htm. The site is in Japanese only. Rotating special exhibits. Past exhibits have featured kimono examples from the Taisho to the Showa era.

The Japan Folk Crafts Museum
4-3-33 Komaba, Meguro-ku, Tokyo
Tel:03-3467-4527

Folk crafts primarily from Japan but incorporating some international pieces as well. It is possible to visit this museum virtually with over 200 pieces from the collection now online, including textiles.
Website: http://www.mingeikan.or.jp/english/

Tokugawa Art Museum
1017, Tokugawa-cho, Higashi-ku, Nagoya
Tel: 81-52-935-6262
Website: http://www.tokugawa-art-museum.jp/english/index.html

Tokyo National Museum
12-9 Ueno Park, Taito-ku
Tel: 03-3822-1111
Website: http://www.tnm.go.jp/en/servlet/Con?pageId=X00&processId=00 This site is also available in German, Korean, Chinese, French and Spanish.
The Honkan Japanese gallery hosts exhibitions on Japanese textiles. Recent exhibits have looked at *ukiyo-e* and costumes from the *Edo* period.

Kyoto and Surrounding Kansai Area
Kobe Fashion Museum
2-9-1 Koyo-cho naka, Higashinada-ku
Kobe, Hyogo
658-0031 Japan
Tel: 81-78-858-0050
Website:http://www.fashionmuseum.or.jp/src/
This site is in Japanese but if you click on the museum link, the admission cost and hours is written in English.
There are examples of fashion from around the world as well as examples of Japanese textiles such as costumes from the *kabuki* theater etc. Displays are changed four to five times a year.

Kodai Yuzen-en Museum
668 Jumonji-cho, Inokuma nishiiru, Takatsuji-dori
Shimogyo-ku, Kyoto
Tel: 075-823-0500

Kyoto National Museum
527 Chayamachi, Higashiyama-ku, Kyoto, Japan 605-0931
Tel: 075-541-1151
Website: http://www.kyohaku.go.jp/eng/index_top.html The site is also available in Chinese, Korean, French and Spanish.
Gallery 14 hosts a permanent textile collection with Japanese textile examples ranging from the theatrical to the religious. The museum has staged special exhibits on children's kimonos and kimonos from the *Edo* period, to name a few.

The Costume Museum
Izutsu Building 5th Floor
Shinhanayacho-Dori Horikawa Higashishiiru
Shimogyo-ku Kyoto 600-8468
Website:http://www.iz2.or.jp/english/index/.html

Life sized dolls are dressed in a variety of costumes.

The Japanese FolkCrafts Museum (Nihon Mingeikan)
4-3-33 Komaba, Meguro-ku
Tel: 03-3467-4527
Website: http://www.mingeikan.or.jp/english/
There is a permanent textile exhibit with many fine examples of kimonos and other textiles.

Okinawa
Okinawa Prefectural Museum
Under construction/Opening for 2007 or 2008
Website:http://www-edu.pref.okinawa.jp/kensetsu/english/index.html

Online Collections of Japanese Art

Asian Art Museum of San Francisco
http://www.asianart.org

Boston Museum of Fine Arts
http://www.mfa.org

British Museum
http://www.thebritishmuseum.ac.uk

Cleveland Museum of Art
http://www.clevelandart.org

Detroit Institute of The Arts
http://www.dia.org

Freer and Sackler Galleries
http://www.asia.si.edu/collections/japanese-Home.htm

Kimball Art Museum
http://www.kimbellart.org

Los Angeles County Museum of Art
http://www.lacma.org/

Marubeni Corporation- kimono collection
http://www.marubeni.com/gallery/kimono/index.html

Metroploitan Museum of New York
http://www.metmuseum.org

Minneapolis Institue of Art
http://www.artsmia.org

Musee Guimet
http://www.museeguimet.fr

Museum of Japanese Traditional Arts Crafts (Nihon GogeiKai)
Website: http://www.nihon-kogeikai.com

Seattle Art Museum
Website:http://www.seattleartmuseum.org

Textile Museum of Canada
Website:http://www.textilemuseum.ca

The Field Museum
Website: http://www.fieldmuseum.org/ The Boone Collection has over 3,500 artifacts from East Asia and some are available to be seen online.

The Textile Museum (Washington DC)
Website:http://www.textilemuseum.org *Special exhibits occasionally feature Japanese textiles.

Victoria and Albert Museum, London, England
Website: http://www.vam.ac.uk/

Please Note: This information was accurate when it was published, but it can change without notice. Please check directly with the facility with regards to hours of operation and admission prices before planning your trip.

Flea Markets in Japan

If the thought of rummaging through hundreds of stalls in hope of finding that special piece for your collection or next sewing project sounds like fun to you, then Japanese flea marketing is a must. With many a market only held once a month or twice a year, a plan is needed before setting out. Many a visitor or even a long time resident has been disappointed after traveling for hours by train to find out that they have the wrong weekend!

Shrines, temples, sports stadiums and even parking lots serve as temporary locations for great bargain hunting. The following short list is of some of the most popular markets. Please keep in mind that popularity does not guarantee an abundance of vintage textiles. Success largely depends on persistence.

Tokyo & Surrounding Kanto Area
Ajinomoto Stadium Flea Market
Location: 376-3 Nishi-cho, Chofu-ku, Tokyo
Time: 10:00-16:00
Access: Tobitakyu station on the Keio Line or Tama-Bochi Mae station on the Seibu Tamagawa Line.
With 600+ stalls selling a variety of goods from produce outside of the gates to comics, key chains and yes kimonos. This is one of the largest flea markets in all of Japan.

Asakusa Sumida Park
Location: Sumida Park, Hanakawado 2, Taito-ku, Tokyo
Time: 10:00-16:00
Access: Near Asakusa station on the Ginza, JR Tobu Line.

A small market more of the draw is the scenery of Asukusa

Ariake Rinkai Fukutohsin Jambo FM
Location: Aomi Nishi temporal car park area, 1 Aomi , Koto-ku Tokyo
Time: 10:00-16:00
Access: Aomi Sta. on the New Transit Yurikamome Line or Tokyo Teleport Sta. Rinkai Fukutoshin.

Arai Yakushi Temple
Location: 5-3-5, Arai, Nakano-ku, Tokyo
Time: First Sunday of every month. The schedule in January changes to the 2nd Sunday of every month.
Access: Araiyakushi-mae Station on the JR Nakano line or Seibu Shinjuku Line.

Heiwajima Antique Festival
Location: Tokyo Ryutsu Center 6-1-1 Heiwajima O-ta-ku Tokyo
Time:10:00-18:00. This market is held 5 times a year.
Access: Tokyo Ryutsu Center on the Tokyo Monorail or Heiwajima on the Keihin Kyuko.

Meiji Park
Kasumigaoka-machi Shinjuku-ku Tokyo
Time: 9:00-15:00. Open Saturdays and Sundays (irregular schedule)
Sendagaya station or Kokuritsu-Kyogiyo on Oedo Line
Website: http://www.otakara.net/ (In Japanese)

Oedo Antique Market
Location:Tokyo International Forum, 3-5-1 Marunochi, Chiyoda-ku, Tokyo
Time: 9:00-4:00. Held on the first and third Sunday of every month
Access:JR Yuracho Station, or Tokyo station / Keio Line
There are more than 250+ stalls with ceramics, kimonos, etc.
Check out the following site for more details.
http://www.antique-market.jp

O-I Keibajo (race track) in No. 1 Parking Area
Location: 2-1-2 Katsushima Shinagawa-ku Tokyo
Time: 9:00-15:00
Access: O-I Keibajo Station or Ekaigawa Station (Keihin Kyu-Ko Line)
With over 600 vendors this a huge market. It is only held two or three times a month.

Roppongi Antique Market
Location:Roppongi Roi Bldg. 5-5-1 Roppongi Minato-ku Tokyo
Time:8:00-17:00. The 4th Thursday of each month.
Access: Roppongi Station Hibiya Station
No website but the number is 03-3583-2081

Shinagawa Flea Market

Shinagawa InterCity Kounan 2-15-2 Minato-ku, Tokyo
Time: 11:00-16:00
Access: South Exit Shinagawa Station JR line

Shinjuku Central Park
Location: Shinjuku Central Park, Nishi-Shinjuku 2-11, Shinjuku-Ku Tokyo
Time: 10:00-16:00
Access: Tosho-mae station on the Toei Oedo Line or Seibu Shinjuku Line (in the back of the Tokyo Metro Government building)
Generally clothing & other household items

Takahata Fudo
Location: Magreg, 1-10-2 Ochiai, Tama-city, Tokyo
Time: 8:00-16:00. Third Sunday of every month.
Access: Takahata Fudo Sta. on the Keio Line
A small market with only 100+ dealers.

Togo Antique Market
Location: Togo Shrine 1-5-3 Jingumae, Shibuya-ku, Tokyo
Time: 4:00-15:00. First, fourth & fifth Sunday
Access: Harajuku Station on JR Line and Meiji-Jingumae on the Chiyoda Line.
Kimonos, yukatas, used clothes etc.

Tokyo Dome Jumbo Flea Market- Tokyo Dome City- Prism City
Location: Tokyo Dome City, 1-3-61 Kouraka Bunkyo-Ku, Tokyo
10:00-16:00
Access: This site is accessible by 3 different train lines. Suido-bashi station on JR line, A2 Suido-bashi station (Toei-Mita), the A-1 exit of Kasuga station (O-edo line) and #1 or 2 exit of Korakuen station (Nanboku, Marunochi lines)

Yokohama Koto World (antique market)
Location: Exhibition Hall D, Pacifico Yokohama 1-1-1 Minotomirai Nishiku, Yokohama-shi, Kanagawa-ken
Time: 12:00-17:00 (special time on the first day) Held twice a year.
Access: Minatomirai Sta. Minatomirai Line, Sakuragicho Sta, (JR Negishi, Toyoko, Yokohama Shiei chikatetsu lines)
This massive antique market is only held twice a year but definitely worth a visit. Tickets are available in advance.

Yokohama Arena
Location:Yokohama Arena, Shin-Yokohama 3-10 Kohoku-ku, Yokohama-shi, Kanagawa-ken
Time: 10:00-16:00
Accesss: 5 minutes from Shin-Yokohama (JR Yokohama line, Yokohama Shiei Chikatetsu subway lines, Tokaido-Shinkansen Line)

Yokohama International Stadium Flea Mar-

ket
Location: Yokohama International Stadium Kozue-cho 3300 Kouhoku-ku Yokohama, Kanagawa
Time: 10:00-16:00
Access: Shin-Yokohama Shiei Chikatetsu lines, or Kozkue-cho on the JR Yokohama line.

Yokohama Marine Tower Sunday Market
Location: Marine Tower 15 Yamashita-cho, Naka-ku Yokohama, Kanagawa
Time: 11:00-17:00. Every Sunday throughout the year.
Access: Motomachi -chukagei on the Mintomirai Line, Kannai station on the JR Negishi line, or Yokohama-shiei on the Chikatetsu Line
Small weekly market.

Yokohama Bayside Flea Market at Pacifico Yokohama Exhibition Hall D
Location: Minato -Mirai 1-1-1 Nishi-ku Yokohama Kanagawa
Time: 10:00-16:00
Access: Minatomirai Station on the Minatomirai line, or Sakuragicho Station on the Tokyo Toyoko, JR Negishi, Yokohama shiei Chikatetsu subway line.

Yoyogi Park
Location: 2 Jinnan Yoyogi-Kamizonocho Shibuya-ku Tokyo
Time: 9:00-16:00
Access: 5 minute walk from Harajuku station on the JR Yamanote line or Meiji Jingu -mae station (Chiyoda-ku),or Shibuya station.

Kyoto
Kitano Tenmangu- Shrine
Time: The 25th of every month
Access: Imadegawa Dori, between Nishi-oji & Senbon take city bus 50 or 101 from JR Kyoto station or 201 from Demachiyanagi station to Kitano Tenmangu-mae
Amazing selection of antique kimonos & ceramics.

To-ji
Website: http://www.touji-ennichi.com/ The site is in Japanese.

Osaka
Ohatsu Tenjin
Time: First Friday of every month
Access: JR Osaka Station
Stalls selling tools, antiques clothing

Shintennoji Taishie
Time: Early morning until 16:30. 21st of each month
Access: Kintetsu Domyo Station or Kyoto station.
Over 600 stalls with ceramics, clothing & gift items.

Online Antique Market Listings

http://www.paperlantern.net
http://www.e-yakimono.net/html/kanto-antiques.htm.
Tokyo Weekender~ http://www.weekender.co.jp/

Textile Associations & Cooperatives

Textile associations and cooperatives are one of the best places to learn about Japanese textiles and meet the people behind them. The following short list is only of a few organizations in major urban centers in Japan. The word in italics after the phone number indicates the type of textile produced and the dyeing method. Please see The Traditional Crafts of Japan website for more information: http://www.kougei.or.jp/english/

Tokyo & Kanto Region
Kihachijo Textile Assocaition
2025 Kashitate, Hachijo-machi, Hachijo-jima, Tokyo
tel:04996-7-0516 (Honba Kihachijo)
Website: http://www.kougei.or.jp/english/crafts/0106/d0106-1.html

Tokyo Order-Made Dyeing Association
3-20-12 Nishi-Waseda, Shinjuku-ku, Tokyo
tel: 03-3208-1512 (Tokyo Somekomon)
Website: http://www.kougei.or.jp/english/crafts/0201/d0201-1.html

Tokyo Yukata Assocaition
3-20-12 Nishi-Waseda, Shinjuku-ku, Tokyo
tel: 03-3208-1521 (Tokyo Somekomon)

Kyoto & Kansai Region
Kyoto Textile Weavers' Cooperative Association
607 Eiraku-cho, Kirya, Gunma Prefecture, Kyoto
tel: 0277-43-7171 (Kiryu Ori Fabrics)

Nishijin Textile Industrial Cooperative
414 Tatemonzen-cho, Imadegawa Minami-iru
Horikawa-dori, Kamigyo-ku, Kyoto
tel: 075-432-6131 (Nishijin Ori)
Website: http://www.nishijin.or.jp/eng/eng.htm

Isesaki Textile Association
31-9 Kuruwa-cho, Isesaki, Gunma Prefecture
tel: 0270-25-2700 (Isesaki Gasuri)

Kyoto Corporation Federation of Dyers and Colorists
481 Toroyama-cho, Shijo-agaru, Nishinotoin-dori, Nakagyo-ku, Kyoto
tel: 075-255-4496 (Kyo Yuzen, Kyo Komono, Kyo Kanako Shibori)

Kyoto Embroidery Association
378-1 Kotake-cho, Matsubara-agaru, Kawaramchio-dori, Shimogyo-ku, Kyoto
tel: 075-361-5495 (Kyo Nui)

Kiryu Textiles Weavers Cooperative Association
5-1 Eiraku-cho, Kiryu, Gunma Prefecture
tel: 0277-43-7171 (Kiryu Ori)

Nagasaki & Kyushu Region
Hakata Textile Industrial Association
1-4-12 Hakataeki-Minami, Hakata-ku
Fukuoka, Fukuoka Prefecture (Kyushu)
tel: 092-472-0761 (Hakata Ori)
Website: http://www.kougei.or.jp/english/crafts/0120/f0120.html

Okinawa
Naha Traditional Textile Association
2-64 Shuritobaru-cho, Naha, Okinawa
tel: 098-887-2746
Website: http://www.kougei.or.jp/english/crafts/0128/f0128.html

Kijoka Abaca Association
1103 Aza Kijoka, Ogimi-son, Kumigami-gun, Okinawa Prefecture
tel: 098-44-3202 (Kijoka no Bashofu)

Yomintanzan Minsaa Association
2974-2 Aza Zakimi, Yomitan-son, Nakagami-gun, Okinawa
tel: 098-958-4674 (Yomintanzan Minsaa)
Website: http://www.kougei.or.jp/english/crafts/0125/f0125.html

Tohoku Region
Oitama Tsumugi Traditional Textile Association
1-1-5 Monto-machi
Tonezawa, Yamagata Prefecture
tel: 0238-23-3525 (Oitama Pongee)
Website: http://www.kougei.or.jp/english/crafts/0101/f0101.html

Fabric Stores

The following is a sample of the stores in Tokyo which specialize in old textiles.
Antique Gallery Meguro
2F, 2-24-18 Kami-osaki
11am-7pm
50 antique stalls

Blue and White
2-9-2 Azabu-Juban
Station: Azabu-Juban exit 4 or exit 3
mon-sat. 10am-6pm

Tokyo Folkcraft and Antique Hall
3-9-5 Minami Ikebukuro
daily, except Thursday, 11am-7pm

Oriental Bazaar
5-9-13 Jingumae Tokyo,
Station: Meji-jingumae or Harajuku or Omtesando
Daily, 7:30-8:30 Wed to Fri. 10am-7pm

Glossary

asanoha~ A six-sided pattern. This regular geometric pattern represents the over lapping of the hemp leaves (asa). It was believed to bring good luck to those who wore the pattern.

bai or **ume**~ It represents purity of character. The plum flower and pine in winter are seen as symbols of good fortune.

chirimen~ The threads are twisted while weaving, creating a wrinkled silk.

gosyo guruma~ An imperial wheel or cart from Heian Period.

Gosho Ningyo~ Ceramic court dolls from the Edo period. The unisex dolls are characterized by white skin, a cute face, small limbs and a big head.

hana-guruma~ A flower cart.

hanabishi~ A diamond pattern with foliated edges.

haniwa ~ Clay sculptures placed on burial grounds. Images included people, boats, homes, instruments etc.

haragake~ A child's bib.

ichimatsu~ A checked pattern composed of two alternating dark and light colors. It was named after the18th century kabuki actor Sanokawa Ichimatsu who wore this pattern.

igeta~ The first character in this word means well. It means a grid pattern.

juban~ nagajuban. A slip, sometimes referred to as 'hidden smartness' worn underneath a kimono. They can be plain or dyed even deep shades of red with exquisite patterns to match.

kaede~ A maple-leaf motif.

kame~ A turtle. The turtle is a symbol of longevity. The belief was that it could live for 10,000 years.

kanoko-shibori~ A tie-dye technique, named for its resemblance to the spotting on a fawn's coat. Fast Fact~ The kanoko dot design on this print fabric is based on the fawn-spot from kanoko-shibori, shibori being a type of dyeing and in this case tie-dye. Kanoko -shibori was one of the most popular textiles in the Edo Period. (Source:Jaanus) Was there a predecessor to this dot design? yes. It was called tsujigahana, which combined tie-dying and hand painting. In the 17th century it declined as it was too costly and labor intensive to make and this led to the development of the kanoko dot design. (Source: Jannus)

kasuri~ A woven fabric with pre-dyed threads. The undyed section becomes the motif.

kicho~ A partition made of cloth used in ancient Japan.

kikko~ Literally translates as a tortoise shell. It is often used as an overall ground pattern. Sometimes it is combined with foliated diamonds and is called kikko-hanabishi. This pattern has been used on textiles since Heian Japan.

kiku~ chrysanthemum. Originally this flower together with paulownia were used on common utensils. By the end of the Kamakura period these motifs were reserved for the emperor's exclusive use.

kinsha~ A silk crepe.

matsuri~ A festival or a holiday.

meisen~ A machine woven silk.

obi~ A belt or long sash for a kimono.

orizuru~ An origami paper crane.

seigaiha~ A semicircular wave pattern resembling fans. The oldest record of this design in Japan was discovered on a female haniwa figure.

sayagata~ A lattice formed from interlocking swastikas.

shakuhachi~ A Japanese flute.

shibori~ A term used to describe several methods of dyeing cloth including tying, binding, folding etc.

Shinto~ The word literally means 'the way of the gods'. It is the indigenous faith of Japan.

sho or **matsu**~ A pine tree. The pine represents endurance, longevity and good fortune.

takarabune~ A treasure ship.

tasuki~ A diamond lattice pattern created by intersecting lines.

take~ bamboo. It represents strength and flexibility. This symbol is often combined with plum and pine. In Japanese this combination of pine, bamboo, and plum is referred to as sho chiku bai. They are considered symbols of good fortune. Sometimes this combination is referred to as 'the three friends.'

tatewaku~ A wave design which resembles an hourglass. It is often used in combination with another motif such as a chrysanthemum (kiku-tatewaku) or a cloud (kumo-tatewaku).

temari~ Traditionally hand-crafted thread balls made from silk kimono remnants. They are thought to bring good fortune.

tombo~ A dragonfly. This is one of Japan's oldest motifs.

tomoe~ A pattern composed of one or three comma like shapes within a circle.

tsuru~ A crane. A crane is a symbol of long life as it was believed that they could live for a thousand years.

tsuzu~ A bell.

tsuzumi ~ A hand drum.

uroko~ A design of wavy lines resembling fish scales.

yabane~ Feathers of an arrow. The yabane motif was first made popular in the 17th century.

yukiwa~ A crystalized snow pattern which looks like small hexagons.

Bibliography

Books

Brandon, Reiko, Fukai, Akiko, Jackson, Anna, Tipston, Elise and Van Assche, Annie. *Fashioning Kimono: Dress and Modernity in Early Twentieth-century Japan.* London, UK:5 Continents, 2005.

Cutler, Thomas W. *A Grammar of Japanese Ornament and Design.* NY, NY: Dover Publications, 2003.

Dalby, Liza. *Geisha.* Berkeley, CA: University of California Press, 1983.

Dalby, Liza. *Kimono: Fashioning Culture.* Seattle, WA: University of Washington Press, 1993.

Gluckman, Dale Carolyn and Takeda, Sharon Sadako. *When Art Became Fashion: Kosode in Edo-Period Japan.* New York, NY: Weatherhill, 1993.

Hibi, Sadao. and Fukuda, Kunio. *The Colors of Japan.* Tokyo, Japan: Kodansha International, 2001.

Hibi, Sadao and Niwa, Motoji. *Snow, Wave, Pine-Traditional Patterns in Japanese Design.* New York, NY: Kodansha America Inc., 2001.

Horn, Diane V. *Japanese Kimono Designs.* Owings Mills, MD: Stemmer House Publishers, 1991.

Imperatore, Cheryl and Maclardy, Paul. *Kimono Vanishing Tradition:* Japanese Textiles of The 20th Century. Atglen, PA: Schiffer Publishing Ltd.

Jackson, Anna. *Japanese Textiles in the Victoria and Albert Museum.* London, England:Victoria and Albert Museum, 2001.

Mizoguchi, Saburo. *Arts of Japan 1: Design Motifs.* New York, NY: Weatherhill, 1973.

Nomura, Shojiro and Ema, Tsutoma. *Japanese Kimono Designs.* Mineola, NY: Dover Publication, 1986.

Ogawa, Yuki. *Sick of Suits, Slipping into something more comfortable.* The Asahi Shimbun. 02/11/2004. http://www.asahi.com/english/lifestyle/TKY200412110131.html

Rathbun, William Jay. *Beyond The Tanabata Bridge: Traditional Japanese Textiles.* London, England: Thames and Hudson, 1993.

Samson, George. *A History of Japan to 1334.* Stanford, California: Stanford University Press, 1958.

Terry, Charles. *Haniwa: As Shown In Four American Museums*, Asia Society, 1960.

Van Riel, Paul. *Kimono: Kimono.* Leiden, Netherlands: Hotei Publishing, 2001.

Verneuil, M.P. *Japanese Silk Designs in Full Color.* Mineola, NY: Dover Publications, 2004.

Yamaguchi, Mari. *Kimono makers turn to computer graphics*, Net sales. USA Today, 9/17/2004. http://www.usatoday.com/tech/news/techinnovations/2004-09-17-digital-kimono_x.htm

Yamanaka, Norio. *The Book of Kimono.* New York, NY: Kondansha America, 1987.

Yang, Sunny and Narasin, Rochelle M. *Textile Art of Japan.* Tokyo, Japan: Japan Publications Trading Company, 2000.

Yasuda, Anita. *Japanese Children's Fabrics.* Atglen, PA: Schiffer Publishing Ltd., 2004.

Yumioka, Katsumi. *Kimono and Colors of Japan.* Tokyo, Japan: PIE Books, 2005.

Websites

Japanese Art and Architecture Users System. 28 August 2006. http://www.aisf.or.jp/~jaanus/

Thompson, Ginny. Temari. 8 Aug. 2006. TemariKai. 22 August http://www.temarikai.com/

McGann, Kass. Reconstructing History. 4-6 August 2006. http://www.reconstructing-history.com/japanese/ancient.html)

Parent, Dr. Mary Neighbour. Japanese Art and architecture Users System. 12-15 August 2006. http://www.aisf.or.jp/~jaanus/